"The aspect of the venerable mansion has always affected me like a human countenance, bearing the traces not merely of outward storm and sunshine, but expressive also of the long lapse of mortal life and accompanying vicissitudes that have passed within."

Nathaniel Hawthorne, *The House of the Seven Gables*, 1851

Windows on the Past

FOUR CENTURIES OF NEW ENGLAND HOMES

JANE C. NYLANDER WITH DIANE L. VIERA

FOREWORD BY WENDELL GARRETT

INTRODUCTION BY CARL R. NOLD

COLOR PHOTOGRAPHS

BY DAVID BOHL

IN APPRECIATION FOR THEIR GENEROSITY AND SUPPORT,

THIS SECOND EDITION IS DEDICATED TO

WILLIAM C. S. AND LUCILE HICKS

HISTORIC NEW ENGLAND

Foreword by Wendell Garrett   9

Windows on the Past: Introduction by Carl R. Nold   12

NEW ENGLAND ON THE MIND 22

CULTIVATING EDEN 43

TIME-HONORED HOUSES 63

ROOMS OF THEIR OWN 85

TIES THAT BIND 109

BACKSTAIRS LIFE 133

COMFORT AND CONVENIENCE 147

AT THE TABLE 173

REMEMBERING THE PAST 192

PRIVATE OWNERSHIP,
PERMANENT PROTECTION 216

Properties of Historic New England   228

Further Reading   234

Acknowledgments   236

Index   238

FOREWORD

opposite

Behind Forest Hall,
the Barrett House in
New Ipswich, New
Hampshire, stands a
Gothic Revival sum-
mer house, built
around 1840. Sited on
top of a terraced hill-
side, it overlooks more
than seventy-five
acres of woods, mea-
dows, and gardens.

"Our ancestors sought a new continent," said James Russell Lowell in 1866. "What they found was a new condition of mind." The Revolution reversed Americans' loyalty to the king of England with astonishing abruptness. As John Adams put it in 1818, "The radical change in the principles, opinions, sentiments, and affections of the people was the real American Revolution." Yet the rejection of Britain was tempered by ambivalence, and it may be that this selective attitude toward the colonial past helps explain the differences between Americans and the English in general and the uniqueness of American architecture and furniture in particular. The national consciousness that flourished in the republic's early years may be interpreted positively as the expression of a cultural identity distinct from England's or negatively as a deplorable example of cultural insularity.

"After the first Cares for the Necessaries of Life are over, we shall come to think of the Embellishments," Benjamin Franklin confidently wrote in 1763. "Already some of our young Geniuses begin to lisp Attempts at Painting, Poetry, and Musick." "Embellishments," as Franklin noted, were replacing mere comfort in the homes of the rich; comfort was supplanting privation in the houses of the not-so-rich. Yeoman farmers, urban craftsmen, and merchants were building a prosperous and productive society. In constructing houses, planning gardens, and painting or carving furniture, these accomplished amateurs followed the latest pattern books from England. In all of those books, design was controlled by the same preoccupation with order and proportion that governs much of the painting, literature, and music of the time. By 1750 coastal towns such as Portsmouth, Boston, and Newport were already miniature Londons. A new society, graceful and cultivated and following the model of western European culture, was being firmly established along with the edge of the North American wilderness as the frontier of forests and Indians was pushed westward. Paradoxically, Europe's colonizing of the New World was doomed by its success: America had been peopled by the most enterprising of Europeans who could innovate at will thanks to the country's isolation. In the act of flourishing, the New England colonies were ceasing to be European.

However, even the most ardent of nationalists had to admit that America was too new, too raw, and too poor to be able to train, teach, or afford artists, writers, and craftsmen working in anything like the style achieved in the Old World. The absence of a long cultural tradition, the lack of patronage, the indifference of the new federal government, and the neglect of classical learning relegated America to the backwater of European artistic and literary achievement. The work of the best colonial artists could not compare with the finish and polish of their British contemporaries such as Gainsborough, Reynolds, Zoffany, and Stubbs. Literature, too, despite a solitary oak like Franklin, was still in the sapling stage compared with Richardson, Addison, Steele, Johnson, and Boswell. While small clusters of enthusiasts corresponded with scientists overseas, no American experimenters could claim discoveries on a par with the epoch-making work being done in Europe. Likewise, no colonial student of society produced anything nearly equal to Adam Smith's *Wealth of Nations* or Denis Diderot's *Encyclopédie.* Even in architecture the Old World influence was overwhelming. Still, it is of some significance that in 1756 the lexicographer Samuel Johnson was talking of an American dialect in speech. And the early architecture and furniture illustrated and discussed in this book demonstrate the ways in which Americans' consciousness of themselves was growing and in which the future was more than implicit. The buildings and objects owned by Historic New England emphasize the divergence of American practice from English models. In these designs we catch the first glimmers of an emerging American style. These New Englanders, urban and rural, even in the diversity of their moods, shared the belief that a new day in human history had dawned.

Walt Whitman once wrote that to understand America one had to appreciate "the pull-down-and-build-over-again spirit" he witnessed in New York City. He was carried away by the restless—and wasteful—national desire to destroy the old and replace it with the new. And it is true: no other nation has so deliberately and repetitively torn down its buildings of architectural importance and monuments of irreplaceable value. It was in the teeth of this sort of avarice and expediency that President Charles W. Eliot of Harvard, with Wendell Phillips, James Russell Lowell, Oliver Wendell Holmes, and others banded together in 1877 to arouse the populace against the wanton destruction of the 1729 Old South Meeting House in Boston—the scene of meetings that fomented the American Revolution. The purchase and preservation of the building in the face of impossible odds was an early source of inspiration to preservationists and antiquarians all over the nation.

A new direction in the preservation of our architectural heritage was heralded by the antiquarian William Sumner Appleton, the founder of the Society for the Preservation of New England Antiquities (now known as Historic New England) in 1910, whose stated purpose was

to save for future generations structures of the seventeenth and eighteenth centuries and the early years of the nineteenth, which are architecturally beautiful and unique, or have special historical significance. Such buildings once destroyed can never be replaced.

During the intervening one hundred years Americans have become convinced that saving old buildings for future generations is a form of progress. Historic New England's diverse, and in many ways unique, buildings and collection vividly reflect the disparate strands of the emerging American culture. There is a functional beauty in these peculiarly American buildings of utility and objects of adornment. Like most men and women, the New Englanders who made and used these things and lived and worked in these structures were caught up in unrelenting and sometimes incomprehensible forces of change. As they moved one foot forward into the future, they left the other firmly planted in the past. Indeed, in their ambivalence, their inconsistency, their capacity for irony, and their expressions of fear and hope, they look singularly familiar to our own age. Historic New England is to be wholeheartedly congratulated for its significant accomplishments and enlightened stewardship in the Northeast over the past century. For "New England is," in the felicitous words of the poet David McCord, "the authorized version of America: her land and people chapter and verse for more than three hundred years."

Wendell Garrett

W INDOWS ON THE PAST

"Built 1737 by Thomas Hancock. Destroyed 1863. The fate of [the John Hancock House] has become a classic in the annals of vandalism. Governor Hancock is said to have intended to bequeath his home to the Commonwealth, but he died without giving effect to this intention by will. In 1859 a strong effort was made to have the Commonwealth purchase the house at a low valuation. This effort failed, and later the heirs offered the house with some of its contents to the city as a free gift, the house to be moved to another site. This plan also failed, and in 1863 the house was destroyed."

William Sumner Appleton,

Bulletin of the Society for the Preservation of New England Antiquities,

May 1910

Eighteenth-century travel accounts document that travelers often visited stately homes during their journeys. George and Martha Washington, for example, frequently welcomed visitors from all walks of life at Mount Vernon. The practice of setting aside houses as museums and historic sites had its origins in America, in fact, at sites associated with Washington and other luminaries of the revolutionary period. The Hasbrouck House in Newburgh, New York, which once served as Washington's headquarters, was established as a historic house museum in 1850. Mount Vernon itself was purchased for preservation in 1860. With the campaign to save the Old South Meeting House, Boston joined the trend of designating historic structures as museums in the 1870s.

Making historic houses into museums is a nineteenth-century concept, which expanded steadily in the twentieth century and reached a peak in the patriotic fervor of the American bicentennial. Communities large and small celebrated two hundred years of American independence by looking closely at their own history and establishing an astonishing number of new museums, many based in historic homes. The "new social history" instilled in Americans the idea that history is more than the story of great leaders and large events. Accounts of everyday life and average people were elevated to new levels of recognition as the foundation on which our modern society is built.

Although the new social history approach was a trend of the 1970s and the 1980s, its ideas found root in the thinking that William Sumner Appleton (1874–1947) brought to the creation of the Society for the Preservation of New England Antiquities (SPNEA) in 1910. Appleton, impassioned by the loss of John Hancock's Boston house in 1863, recognized the value of "lesser antiquities" and the need to preserve common objects that, unlike stellar survivors of periods past, were not then considered to have historical importance. Appleton's diaries and correspondence reveal that his motivations were complex, and indeed they were aimed in part at preserving the Anglo-Saxon, Yankee buildings, artifacts, and ways of life he viewed as threatened by the large influx of new immigrants beginning to fill Boston's neighborhoods. Appleton apparently never seriously considered acquiring a Victorian building or a more modern one for his organization, even though he himself could not resist collecting brand-new objects that he saw as documents of life in his own day with potential for future importance. Although he never held a driver's license, he assembled a large collection of early automobile advertisements as well as art pottery, early-twentieth-century clothing and furnishings, photographs, and postcards. The buildings

pages 12–13

The handblown glass of a window at the Gilman Garrison House in Exeter, New Hampshire, offers a glimpse of the doorway beyond. The house itself serves as a window into the lives of its varied occupants over three centuries, from its original owner, John Gilman, who built a fortified house to protect his newly established wealth, to William Perry Dudley, who restored it in the 1950s.

were more limited in scope than Historic New England (as SPNEA is now known) currently holds, but what Appleton accomplished was the creation of an organization dedicated to the preservation of buildings, landscapes, artifacts, images, documents, and stories representing New England's strong regional character and traditions, with a special focus on domestic life.

The organization's approach to historic buildings changed over time. As late as the mid-1950s, Appleton's successors discarded some furnishings of the Victorian era and later periods. Within fifteen years, however, the pendulum had swung back, and Henry Bowen's 1846 Gothic Revival Roseland Cottage in Woodstock, Connecticut, and Walter and Ise Gropius's 1938 Bauhaus-inspired house in Lincoln, Massachusetts, joined the collection, along with their entire contents.

Having owned 104 properties over its one-hundred-year existence, Appleton's organization reached its centennial in 2010. It survived the Great Depression and World War II—times when the care of buildings presented particular challenges of funds and materials—and emerged in the postwar period as a leader in establishing preservation standards that were adopted nationwide. In the years following the bicentennial, attendance at historic house museums and history museums generally began a steady decline. Museum professionals are still trying to understand this seeming diminishment of interest in history, but among the reasons considered are declines in the teaching of history to young people in schools and increasingly isolated individual activities in the computer age that replace the group interactions and social activities inherent in museum visits. Contributing factors may include changing demands on family time as both parents work and elimination of "blue laws," which used to give museums a privileged place in family activities on Sunday. Some people also point to museums' own failures to accommodate those who are truly interested in history, to open the doors to new audiences, and to present engaging programs for a variety of age and interest groups.

Technology is now enabling virtual museum visits and social networking, bringing places, artifacts, and interactions with those holding common interests into one's

home or headset. Do the library, the museum, and the historic house, some ask, continue to have value in such a world? Have these institutions, conceived largely in the nineteenth century, now outlived their usefulness? Why do we preserve historic houses in the twenty-first century?

By the mid-1970s, Appleton's successors were also struggling with the challenge of a preservation organization that owned too many houses and had insufficient resources for their care and use. New England is rich in surviving buildings from earlier periods, and arguments can be made for preserving even more of them as museums. Directors Abbott Lowell Cummings and Nancy Coolidge were charged with finding new ways to preserve historic houses other than as museums, establishing criteria for the organization's ownership of houses. Dr. Cummings sought to look at buildings in three ways. First of all, he sought to identify properties for the collection that offered the widest educational opportunities. "For any significant museum/educational program," he commented, "institutional ownership rather than adaptive use is mandatory." A second factor was architectural importance, which flows from the educational role. Dr. Cummings and his colleagues sought the creation of a collection of buildings that represent the "variety of types, and an impressive qualitative range" of New England architecture over time, illustrating its breadth and scope, and including buildings that are important as examples of their kind. The third criterion was "total preservation." This was defined as a full awareness of the importance of the building, the landscape, the accumulation of furnishings, and subsequent changes that in turn represent the changing tastes of each generation. In other words, the organization sought to preserve in institutional ownership those houses that came down as totally unspoiled—intact in building, context, contents, and compelling story.

So the question, why do we preserve historic houses? came to be examined for educational value first, as determined by outstanding architectural merit or regional historical significance. Some houses preserved intact are the best surviving examples of classic architectural features and interiors widely used in New England. Others were so rare that they would be endangered if held privately in continued use. Having significant in-depth collections related to a building's overall history added to the educational value. Being part of a story extending beyond the building and contents to help visitors understand the larger stories of New England's history and development confirmed that a house was worthy of being preserved as a museum for the public's benefit.

This evolution of thinking—from looking at buildings individually (often in time of crisis) to creating a system of house museums as an educational tapestry—was the most important step in defining the practices that have been employed for the last thirty years in the management of Historic New England's historic properties. With a collection of properties as the goal, scholars and interpreters can move beyond the value of any one historic place to begin to tell much larger stories about the character of New England, its development over time and across geographic boundaries, and its contributions to the nation and the world. In this way, the potential of historic houses to contribute to our understanding of our society is greatly increased.

The question remains, however, whether one might just as readily study and learn from virtual houses, online images, and interactive stories presented in some computerized form. Is there value in preserving the authentic original? History shows that technologies developed over the centuries have not diminished the human desire to personally experience the authentic. The development of books did not diminish the desire to travel the world; it enhanced knowledge of the opportunities. The creation of photography and television did not deter visits to zoos and museums holding the original subjects of the images and programs. We know from researchers and collectors that even the highest-quality documentation often fails to record every aspect of the original, thus requiring a personal examination of the authentic artifact or document. In an increasingly virtual world, we can only surmise that the original place, building, landscape, or object will become even more highly valued as the source document and that visits to the source will continue to have value no matter what technology brings.

This emphasis on authenticity means, however, that only the best preserved, unaltered, well-researched, and truly original will merit attention. For its collection of historic houses, Historic New England has developed a philosophy of preserving the original fabric, the authentic appearance, the actual artifacts, and all related documentation. During its first fifty years, the organization's aim was to preserve buildings of the seventeenth and eighteenth centuries. Standard practice during this time was to remove later additions and evidence of successive architectural changes (although restoration work was carefully documented through photographs and field notes). A new approach was initiated with the 1969 acquisition of the Codman House in Lincoln, Massachusetts, which had been altered and expanded at least four times since 1740 and contained furnishings, paintings, clothing, photographs, and manuscripts spanning more than two centuries. That year the organization adopted a policy of keeping buildings and their contents intact, retaining all the evidence of

opposite

The dining room of the Phillips House in Salem, Massachusetts, shows the results of the 1911–12 Colonial Revival remodeling, when Victorian embellishments were replaced with decorative elements reminiscent of the Federal period.

changes, new ideas, and various personalities that had left their imprint through the years, rather than recreating what the buildings may have looked like when first constructed. This philosophy seeks to present life exactly as it was, good and bad—not life as we today imagine it might have been.

As Historic New England embarks on its second century, the commitment to creating a wide-ranging collection of historic houses remains strong. This means that the collection must change over time. Since the first edition of this book was published in 2000, we have acquired a thirty-sixth historic house museum, the Stephen Phillips House of Salem, Massachusetts, which tells a largely twentieth-century story. Other additions will undoubtedly follow as the organization seeks to preserve a diverse sampling of New England architecture, periods, and stories. Houses representing both the extraordinary and the common experience must be included.

With a focus on the most authentic preserved houses, other houses that have some but not all the qualities essential to inclusion in the collection offer significant benefits to their communities and should also be preserved for the future. How this is accomplished has evolved. We no longer view creation of a historic house museum as the only, or even the best, way to preserve a special place. Since the 1980s Historic New England has been a leader in considering alternative means of protecting historic buildings. European countries provided some of the models. Just by virtue of age, most European cities have many more historic houses to save than do American cities, but the preserved buildings for the most part are not museums. They continue in active use for their original purpose or are adaptively and sensitively reused in ways that maintain a community's vitality. They contribute to the tax rolls, they are maintained by people who love them, and although privately owned they are still recognized and valued as parts of community heritage. Some public tools protect such buildings that are not museums, from historic districts and design review commissions to carefully written and well-enforced zoning laws.

Historic New England uses its stewardship easement program to preserve non-museum buildings, currently protecting about seventy-five privately owned historic properties. This program places preservation restrictions on a building, which the organization will hold and enforce forever. Over the first hundred years of its history, 104 properties were owned by Historic New England, even though today just thirty-six of them are house museums. The others have been successfully returned to nonmuseum uses but are still fully protected, contribute to our understanding of New England life, and enhance their communities. The easement program (see pages 216–27) offers an alternative to institutional ownership that allows us to concentrate our energies and resources on the most authentic buildings that have the most compelling stories, that will draw public interest and merit public support, as well as on those buildings that do not lend themselves to adaptive use and can be preserved only as museums. This latter group includes many seventeenth-century buildings that are so rare and fragile that they cannot be adapted to other purposes.

Historic New England also owns more than 110,000 artifacts closely associated with New England families or artisans, half on view in the historic properties and the rest carefully preserved and available for formal exhibition, research, and publication. Our library now contains more than one million historic images and other primary materials in the form of books, manuscripts, photographs, negatives, postcards, stereocards, daguerreotypes, architectural drawings, and illustrated ephemera. The

Internet now provides an opportunity to make these rich collections accessible to people around the world, increasing the impact of the organization far beyond anything William Sumner Appleton could have imagined.

The very best historic houses welcome us to experience the authentic, preserved, and documented evidence of the past in ways that the virtual cannot provide. Memorable, transformative experiences with an authentic place or artifact give us a unique understanding and appreciation of the world and the people around us that cannot be found in other ways. When historic houses are doing their jobs well, they provide these transformative experiences. This book draws on the century-long efforts of Historic New England to introduce you to some of the ways in which this collection of historic houses provides authentic experiences. It is an invitation to visit and experience for yourself some of New England's best preserved historic homes. To open the door into one of these houses is to encounter their lives, reflecting both their individuality and the commonality of human experience. In the pages that follow, Jane Nylander and Diane Viera open the doors—and windows—into these houses that do so much to document the breadth and depth of New England's character.

Carl R. Nold, President and CEO
Historic New England

ℕEW ENGLAND ON THE MIND

"Nature has been bountiful to our land

and we need but the hand of art, skillfully applied,

to render it more lovely and more fruitful."

Christopher Gore (1758–1827), creator of Gore Place (1806) in Waltham, Massachusetts

pages 22–23

Little's Lane at the
Spencer-Peirce-Little
Farm in Newbury,
Massachusetts.

this page and opposite

The Hamilton House,
its gardens, and the
adjacent Vaughan
Woods on the Salmon
Falls River in South
Berwick, Maine.

"The cold is merely superficial; it is the summer still at the core, far, far within."

Henry David Thoreau, journal entry, January 12, 1855

"What I admire
and love is
the generous and
spontaneous
[New England]
soil which flowers
and fruits in all
seasons."

Ralph Waldo
Emerson, undated
journal entry

right

A garden sculpture
at the Codman
Estate in Lincoln,
Massachusetts.

opposite

Spring beauty at
the Governor John
Langdon House
in Portsmouth,
New Hampshire.

"I praise the flower-barren fields, the clouds, the tall

Unanswering branches where the wind makes sullen noise.

I praise the fall: it is the human season."

Archibald MacLeish, "Immortal Autumn," 1930

opposite

A pasture scene at the Watson Farm in Jamestown, Rhode Island.

top left

Tools for productive agriculture and ornamental horticulture at the Lyman Estate in Waltham, Massachusetts.

top right

The tidal Salmon Falls River below the Hamilton House in South Berwick, Maine.

right

Relic stone walls still bounding a field at the Codman Estate in Lincoln, Massachusetts.

"[T]he lower hall is very fine, with an archway dividing it, and panelings of all sorts, and a great door at each end, through which the lilacs in front and the pensioner plum-trees in the garden are seen exchanging bows and gestures."

Sarah Orne Jewett,
Deephaven, 1877

right

Garlic grown for the Community Supported Agriculture Program at the Casey Farm in Saunderstown, Rhode Island.

opposite

A welcoming door and entry hall at the Barrett House in New Ipswich, New Hampshire.

opposite

The stairway at
Castle Tucker in
Wiscasset, Maine.

right

Stairs to the gallery
at the Rocky Hill
Meeting House, Ames-
bury, Massachusetts.

below

The staircase
at the Gropius
House in Lincoln,
Massachusetts.

"A kind of old
Hobgoblin Hall,

Now somewhat
fallen to decay,

With weather-
stains upon the
wall,

And stairways
worn, and crazy
doors,

And creaking and
uneven floors,

And chimneys
huge, and tiled
and tall."

**Henry Wadsworth
Longfellow, prelude,
"Tales of a Wayside
Inn," 1863**

"I love it, I love it;
and who shall dare

To chide me for
loving that old
arm-chair?

I've treasured it
long as a sacred
prize;

I've bedewed
it with tears,
and embalmed it
with sighs;

'Tis bound by
a thousand bands
to my heart;

Not a tie will
break, not a link
will start.

Would ye learn
the spell? a mother
sat there,

And a sacred
thing is that old
arm-chair."

Eliza Cook,
"The Old Arm-Chair,"
Godey's Lady's Book,
March 1855

right

The sinuous curves
of a Grecian sofa
in the parlor of the
Marrett House in
Standish, Maine.

below

Plain paper with
a swag border in
the dining room
of the Otis House
in Boston.

opposite

Scenic wallpaper
in the dining room
of the Barrett House
in New Ipswich,
New Hampshire.

"I was dazzled
by the brilliancy
of the room. . . .
The furniture
was exceedingly
rich. . . . [I]t struck
me that here was
the fulfilment of
every fantasy of
an imagination
revelling in various
methods of costly
self-indulgence
and splendid ease.
Pictures, marbles,
vases,—in brief,
more shapes of
luxury than there
could be any
object in enumer-
ating, except for an
auctioneer's adver-
tisement. . . ."

Nathaniel Hawthorne,
*The Blithedale
Romance*, 1852

above

Plasterwork with
neoclassical details in
the ballroom of the
Lyman Estate in Wal-
tham, Massachusetts.

right

This richly carved
mantel in the library
of the Phillips House
in Salem, Massachu-
setts, was likely
carved by Samuel
McIntire or his son.

"There was a large cabinet holding all the small curiosities and knick-knacks there seemed to be no other place for,—odd china figures, and cups and vases, unaccountable Chinese carvings and exquisite corals and sea shells, minerals and Swiss wood-work, and articles of *vertu* from the South Seas."

Sarah Orne Jewett, *Deephaven*, 1877

opposite

The toolshed's upper story and the barn attic at Castle Tucker in Wiscasset, Maine (top left and right). The Phillips House's carriage house in Salem, Massachusetts (bottom left). The attic of the Codman House in Lincoln, Massachusetts (bottom right).

left

Dolls and toys at the Hamilton House in South Berwick, Maine.

"Every day a
new picture is
painted and
framed, held up
for half an hour,

in such lights as
the Great Artist
chooses, and then
withdrawn, and
the curtain falls.

And then the sun
goes down, and
long the afterglow
gives light.

And then the
damask curtains
glow along the
western window.

And now the
first star is lit,
and I go home."

Henry David Thoreau,
as quoted in
*Autumn: A New
England Journey* (1988)

above

A sieve, a shovel, and
a coffee grinder in the
buttery at the Coffin
House in Newbury,
Massachusetts.

opposite

Inscribed graffiti
on a gallery pew at
the Rocky Hill Meet-
ing House in Ames-
bury, Massachusetts.

CULTIVATING EDEN

"A village on a hill, white houses facing on a green, tall elms arching overhead, and a white church spire pointing heavenward: for many Americans this picture represents stability, tradition, national roots, and a retreat from urban stress."

Alan Emmet, *So Fine a Prospect: Historic New England Gardens*, 1996

pages 42–43

The quintessential
New England village
of Wiscasset, Maine,
seen from the front
steps of Castle
Tucker, typifies early
New Englanders'
efforts to turn the
land into compact
town centers and tidy
farms. These architec-
tural features are now
considered icons of
the American identity.

left

The exceptionally
large barn at the
Spencer-Peirce-Little
Farm in Newbury,
Massachusetts, built
in the eighteenth
century and still used
today, testifies to the
farm's productivity.

opposite

An aerial view of
Cogswell's Grant in
Essex, Massachusetts,
reveals the farm's
layout: the barn
(left), its equipment
shed and milk room,
and the kitchen
garden beyond; the
house (right) with its
private dooryard;
the farmyard with its
1700s barn; and
pastures and hay-
fields leading to the
salt marsh and the
Essex River.

Throughout New England's history, the land has been continually reworked and the landscape changed in response to human needs and available resources. The efforts of the first English settlers in the New World in the seventeenth century resulted in an alluring countryside and town centers with characteristic architectural features now considered icons of national identity.

From Maine to Rhode Island, Historic New England's 1,350 acres of landscape tell the stories of people who made their living from the land and of others who created intimate gardens as a means of personal expression or who built grand pleasure grounds to showcase their prosperity. Most of these landscapes reveal changing methods of agricultural practices and tastes in garden design as well as natural maturation. In New England today historic landscapes that have remained undivided and have been cared for since the seventeenth century are rare, especially large tracts of farmland. Historic New England, however, preserves the larger part of four such farms: Cogswell's Grant and the Spencer-Peirce-Little Farm in Essex County, Massachusetts, and the Watson and Casey Farms in southern Rhode Island.

At the Casey Farm in Saunderstown, Rhode Island, more than three hundred acres stretching from Narragansett Bay to the Pettaquamscutt River were owned by the Casey family from 1702 to 1955. After an initial period of personal prosperity, which ended with the decline of nearby Newport following the Revolutionary War, the Casey family employed tenant farmers who raised cranberries, corn, and potatoes. Family members, who pursued careers in business, the military, engineering, and architecture, retained two rooms in the farmhouse for their own use during the summer. Throughout the nineteenth century the farm remained a firm center and symbol for the Caseys, the unchanging place to which they returned each year to renew their ties to the land and to one another.

Thomas Lincoln Casey, brigadier general and chief of the U.S. Army Corps of Engineers, especially cherished the family homestead and spent his summers researching the farm's history. In his "Historical Sketch of Casey Farm" (1881), he expressed the farm's symbolic value: "[A]s an heir-loom for the preservation of which many sacrifices have been made by my ancestors and as a repository of the ashes of my beloved kindred, the place is beyond price, and I trust will ever be zealously guarded and cherished by me and mine." In 1955 his son Edward Pearce Casey bequeathed the farm to Historic New England, stipulating that it always remain a working farm, as it has.

right

At the Codman Estate in Lincoln, Massachusetts, the "ha-ha" wall built by John Codman still stands. The "octagon" meadow below it was replaced by a smaller meadow and a pond in the 1860s, when extensive improvements were made to the estate.

Most New England farms have not been blessed with the extensive acreage, rich soil, and ocean-tempered climate of Historic New England's large farms. Most were closer to one hundred acres, and New England farmers have always struggled with thin, rocky soil, the challenges of a short growing season, and unpredictable extremes of weather. One of the first organized efforts to improve farm productivity occurred in 1792, when the Massachusetts Society for Promoting Agriculture (MSPA) was formed by some of Boston's leading citizens to disseminate information and encourage experimentation in crop rotation, new fertilizers, selective breeding, and other progressive techniques. In that decade the merchant John Codman, a founding member and trustee of MSPA, acquired a 450-acre country seat in Lincoln, Massachusetts, and planned an ambitious renovation of the house, grounds, and farm operations.

While on business in England in 1800, Codman carefully observed the parklike views, ornamental gardens, and productive farmland of large English estates. From abroad he sent orders that new trees be planted to conceal the barns and the public road in front of his house in Lincoln. On his return he built a new house for the hired farm agent, new barns, wells, and an up-to-date drainage system to support the farm's agricultural activity. Codman was as interested in the property's ornamental landscape as in its improved agricultural practices, planting trees and separating the agricultural landscape from the cultivated area in front of the house with a nearly invisible retaining wall known as a "ha-ha" wall. The response to his efforts delighted him: his wife's sophisticated cousin, Rebecca Gore—the wife of the Massachusetts governor Christopher Gore, who lived in nearby Waltham in another grand house—called the Codman Estate "the handsomest place in America."

The six-hundred-foot-long peach wall at the Lyman Estate in Waltham, Massachusetts, is more than an architectural feature to screen the farm's working areas. Eleven feet high, the brick partition was built primarily to shelter and support the peach and other fruit trees espaliered to grow against it.

left

Alvan Fisher's 1820 watercolor of Theodore Lyman's estate, called The Vale, shows both the house, designed by Samuel McIntire in 1793, and the picturesque landscape beginning to reach maturity.

opposite bottom

Bountiful spring daffodils emerge early in the reflected warmth of the peach wall. Riches inside the Lyman greenhouses include century-old camellia trees and huge grapevines grown from a scion brought from Hampton Court in England.

In 1793, at the same time that John Codman began enhancing his lands in Lincoln, Theodore Lyman, another prosperous merchant and MSPA member, was working with William Bell, a gardener and nurseryman from England, to design the pleasure grounds of his newly constructed house in nearby Waltham, Massachusetts. The Vale, as Lyman named it, was one of the first New England landscapes laid out in the eighteenth-century English picturesque style and is the earliest and most extensive of its type to remain nearly intact today.

Like the setting of an English country house, the Lyman Estate features large pleasure grounds with expanses of grass and unobstructed views, carefully sited specimen trees, wide meandering pathways, a deer park (although the deer are gone), and ponds formed by a dammed brook. Lyman's interest in technological innovation and rare plants was also evident in his greenhouses, among the earliest in the country still in operation today. Here Lyman and his staff raised camellias and other ornamental plants as well as exotic table fruits such as lemons and pineapples.

Not all newly prosperous New England merchants in the Federal period emulated the picturesque English landscape style. In 1807 thirty-six-year-old James Rundlet, a successful merchant, began constructing an imposing three-story house and laying out its extensive grounds in the heart of Portsmouth, New Hampshire. Carefully planned, Rundlet's garden is one of the oldest in the city to retain its original configuration.

Like many other wealthy New Englanders of the time, Rundlet believed that at least some of his land should be productive. Although his home was located in the center of Portsmouth, a portion of the family's food—vegetables, small fruits, pork and beef, and dairy products—was raised right there. Rundlet also owned a larger working farm on Sagamore Creek, just outside the city, where commercial crops were grown, as well as hay and grain to feed the cows, pigs, and carriage horses kept in town. Rundlet's property was laid out in a grid plan, with straight paths delineating clear distinctions among its various uses: stable yard, cow yard, garden, and orchard. This conservative plan varied greatly from the more picturesque English-inspired estates of Codman and Lyman, showing that changes in landscape taste were slow to affect those not close to Boston.

Further removed from the influence of agricultural reformers and picturesque gardeners were the many other New Englanders who continued to struggle to provide for their families from the land. Even a minister such as Daniel Marrett of Standish, Maine, spent a part of each day engaged in agricultural activity, growing grain, vegetables, and fruit and keeping livestock for meat and milk for his immediate family. Some people turned to specialty crops, such as sheep or apples, but others continued in the old ways. In appearance, many of these farms reflected their old-fashioned point of view: little attention was given to ornamental planting or landscape design. Barren dooryards, pecked by chickens, were cluttered with the scattered debris that rewards today's historical archaeologist. By the 1830s and 1840s much of the landscape within one hundred miles of Boston had been deforested for firewood, and hundreds of families began to desert their unproductive hill farms for the greener pastures of New York, Ohio, and the other new states carved from the Northwest Territory. Populations had peaked in 1820 in towns such as New Ipswich, New Hampshire, and Standish, Maine. From then on, the upland New England landscape also featured deserted farmhouses and regrowth of forests.

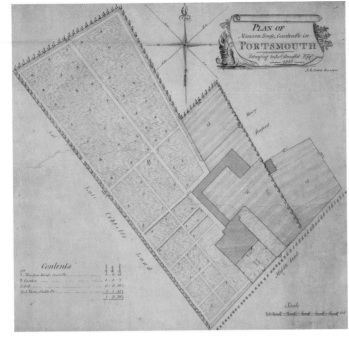

Life began to change in the 1830s with a new emphasis on domesticity and rural beautification, the principles of which were codified in Andrew Jackson Downing's *A Treatise on the Theory and Practice of Landscape Gardening Adapted to North America with a View to the Improvement of Country Residences* (1841). This trend-setting book, America's first guide to new styles in landscape design, was quick to have an impact. In it Downing gave a compelling rationale for investing time, money, and labor in the beautification of one's home and garden. "The love of country is inseparably connected with the *love of home*," he wrote, "… and there is no employment or recreation which affords the mind greater or more permanent satisfaction, than that of cultivating the earth and adorning our own property…. In rendering his home more beautiful, [a homeowner] not only contributes to the happiness of his own family, but improves the taste, and adds loveliness to the country at large."

These words may have struck a chord with Henry Chandler Bowen, an active abolitionist, Congregationalist, and Republican living in Brooklyn, New York, who built a Gothic Revival summer retreat for his family in his hometown of Woodstock, Connecticut, in 1846. Like the Caseys, Bowen believed that his family could absorb the traditional values of New England's earlier, admired agricultural society by returning to his hometown each summer. From the start Bowen placed equal weight on the design of both the new house and the grounds, and he began planting on the property before the house was completed.

Bowen painted his summer home pink and named it Roseland Cottage after his love of roses, some of which still bloom on the property. Family records show that Bowen frequented the Raspberry Hill Nursery in nearby Brooklyn, Connecticut, and relied on its proprietor, Henry A. Dyer, not only to supply plants and trees for Roseland Cottage but also to supervise the work being done there. Dyer is known to have worked on the imposing boxwood garden, with its six hundred yards of boxwood edging and twenty small flower beds, thought to be one of the oldest surviving boxwood parterres in New England. The Roseland Cottage grounds in Bowen's day also featured an extensive orchard of apples, peaches, cherries, pears, plums, nectarines, grapes, quinces, and currants.

above

A picturesque garden house adds charm to Roseland Cottage in Woodstock, Connecticut. The parterre garden is edged with its original boxwood, laid out in the 1850s.

left

Henry Chandler Bowen loved roses, planting them lavishly around his aptly named home. To celebrate the American centennial, he donated a public park to Woodstock, filling it too with roses and trees. Close by, it still attracts visitors.

opposite top

Following a ten-
year sojourn in
France, the Codmans
returned to Lincoln,
Massachusetts, to
take up life at The
Grange. The house
and its elegant setting
inspired Sarah Cod-
man's watercolors.

Bowen's descendants enjoyed their summers at Roseland Cottage for many years—until 1970, when the property was purchased by Historic New England. In Lincoln, Massachusetts, John Codman had also hoped that his descendants would share his love for their country home, but soon after his sudden death in 1803 his son divided and sold the property. For sixty years the house and grounds were sorely neglected. Then, in 1862, Codman's grandson, Ogden, purchased the property, which he named The Grange, and devoted himself to remodeling and restoring the stately house and grounds, improving the farm's productivity, and reestablishing the place as a summer retreat for his family.

In 1863 Codman reconstructed the retaining wall in front of the house, built a new barn, converted the "octagon" meadow into a hayfield and pond, planted vegetables, fruit trees, and berry bushes, and purchased hens, pigs, dairy cattle, workhorses, and sporting ponies. Most of his efforts were focused on agricultural improvements rather than ornamental landscaping, but seed orders for some flower gardens give a hint of sweet scents and brilliant color. He also planted a large number of evergreen trees and weeping willows, freely arranging them over the lawns where eighteenth-century specimens of elms and two noble tamaracks remained standing. Codman's improvements at The Grange, however, were halted by the great Boston fire of 1872, which destroyed most of his extensive real estate holdings there and eliminated the related rental income. The family left New England and spent the next decade living in France while leasing The Grange to tenants, who slowly let the property deteriorate again.

After the Codman family returned to live permanently at The Grange, the gardens were designed and cared for by Ogden's wife, Sarah, their son Ogden Jr., and their daughter Dorothy. In 1899 Sarah began work on an elaborate two-year project to create a walled Italian garden in a hollow on the northwest side of the house. Ogden Jr., who became a noted architect and interior decorator, may have designed his mother's garden, with its fountain, canal, pergolas, and statuary. No detailed plan has been found, but the skillful use of diminishing perspective to increase the apparent length of the garden reflects a talented hand. Its sense of order and classical restraint contrast sharply with John Codman's surviving picturesque landscape outside the garden walls.

Dorothy Codman helped tend the Italian garden and created an outdoor space of her own that reflected the Colonial Revival taste popular at the turn of the century— an informal cottage garden with a profusion of old-fashioned flowers and a carefully planned sequence of bloom. An interpretation of its colonial predecessors, it was not a pure re-creation, for in it she used unusual plant materials that were not available in earlier times.

*opposite
bottom left*

Like her mother,
Dorothy Codman
made gardening an
important part of her
life, not only tending
Sarah's formal garden
but also creating an
informal cottage
garden for herself.

*opposite
bottom right*

The Codmans' formal
garden, although
rather modest in size,
is quite sophisticated
in design. Sarah
Codman never con-
sidered the garden
complete but continu-
ally worked on it,
adding plants and
revising the border.

far right

Today visitors to
the Hamilton House
in South Berwick,
Maine, can enjoy
concerts in the
garden, which still
offers a splendid view
of the Salmon Falls
River and the adja-
cent Vaughan Woods.
In recent years the
stone walls have been
restored and the elms
replanted along the
house's riverbank.

right

During the 1880s the
Hamilton House was
home to the Goodwin
family, who farmed
the land. The large
barn on the right
occupies the site later
chosen by the Tysons
for their Colonial
Revival garden.

The impact of the Colonial Revival style can be seen even more strongly in South Berwick, Maine, where in 1898 Emily Tyson and her stepdaughter, Elise, bought the Hamilton House and 110 acres overlooking the Salmon Falls River at the urging of the author Sarah Orne Jewett. When Col. Jonathan Hamilton purchased thirty acres here in 1783 and built his handsome Georgian house shortly after, the grounds were soon abuzz with the activity of his international shipping and shipbuilding business. Wharves and warehouses along the shoreline immediately below the house were noisy and often disorderly. There is no evidence of early ornamental pleasure grounds or gardens at the top of the bluff near the house itself, and after Hamilton's death in 1802 the land was used for farming, an apple orchard, and a sheep pasture of declining productivity throughout the nineteenth century.

Inspired by a romantic vision of the colonial past, the later owners Emily and Elise Tyson devoted their considerable resources to restoring and embellishing the house and grounds, working with the Boston architect Herbert Browne and the artist George Porter Fernald. After construction of terraces close to the house, the main perennial garden was begun in 1901 on the site of the old barn, which they had moved out of sight. The Tysons' new "colonial" garden was entered through an arched gateway at the foot of the steps from the house, which led to a path that offered views of the garden, surrounding fields, and adjacent woodland. The garden's dominant feature was a rectangle surrounded by a vine-covered pergola incorporating several seating areas and a small garden room. At the intersection of the main garden paths was a sundial; statues, benches, and other garden features accented the flower beds. Over the years the garden evolved and changed, reflecting the owners' new horticultural interests, their trip to Italy in 1905, suggestions from friends and visitors, and the impact of severe winters and damaging storms.

The care that New Englanders took in placing their houses, designing landscape features, and conserving the natural environment has set a standard. When the Bauhaus architect Walter Gropius accepted a teaching appointment at Harvard University in 1937, he was given a piece of land on which to build a house in Lincoln, Massachusetts, less than two miles from the Codman Estate. Although Gropius designed a modern house, he took a traditional New England approach to its placement: it faces south, set on top of a small hill where there had once been an apple orchard. Seeking to integrate the house into the landscape, Walter and Ise Gropius planned a "civilized area" with a lawn that would serve as an extension of the living area but extend only twenty feet around the house. Beyond this was a second level with fields, an orchard, a meadow, and, beyond, a wetland left in its natural state. Carefully placed trees were added to the landscape as focal points and to provide shade, and bittersweet and grapevines were added.

Like many homeowners of past centuries, the Gropiuses did their own landscaping, taking great care and time with it. Even before construction began, they planted mature trees in locations that would provide shade in summer and color year-round. Stone walls separated the lawn areas from the more natural landscapes, and the Gropiuses added trellises with climbing roses and hardy perennials around the yard so they could enjoy bloom throughout the warm season. The goal was to integrate the interior and exterior spaces.

Despite the difficulties imposed by soil and climate, the New England landscape has been enhanced by talented people who have practiced agriculture and created gardens that serve as refuges and sources of delight. Historic New England's diverse landscapes and gardens testify to differing levels of skill and interest, varied amounts of resources, and the changing tastes of successive owners. Even today, these landscapes offer the endless challenge of trying to control nature and preserve historic design as well as the satisfaction of creating productive crops and vistas of great beauty.

left

The landscape surrounding the Gropius House in Lincoln, Massachusetts, like the house itself, reflects maximum efficiency and simplicity of design. The four acres include modest lawns near the house, a small Japanese garden, specimen trees, and an apple orchard, all framed by the house's generous windows.

*T*IME-HONORED HOUSES

"Clapboards and brick, wood-frame construction and the demands of the New England climate form a regional tradition which was made a part of the design [of our house]; but it is not a dry imitation of what has been in the past. . . . The Old Colonial tradition of a central hall is pleasant and appropriate today. It eliminates corridors, and from it we can reach every room. The clapboard is a time-honored material, used in the region over a hundred years."

Walter and Ise Gropius, "Time Mellows This Modern House,"
House and Garden, January 1949

The Gropius House in Lincoln, Massachusetts, successfully fuses traditional New England design features—clapboards, a welcoming fireplace, a central hall, and wide, south-facing windows—with such functionalist Bauhaus principles as a flat roof, undecorated surfaces, and the use of industrial components.

I t was important to both Walter and Ise Gropius that their first house in America reflect local traditions of form and function, so they spent a season driving through the Massachusetts countryside, studying its architecture and photographing buildings before beginning construction. The Gropiuses admired traditional New England farmhouses, for both their simple forms and functionality as well as for their integration into the landscape. With these lessons in mind, Walter Gropius began designing their new house, carefully combining the modern Bauhaus design philosophies for which he was already famous with the characteristics of older New England architecture they had observed.

Gropius's respect for the architecture of the past was evident in his use of traditional construction forms and materials: clapboards, a brick chimney, a fieldstone foundation, and a fireplace. Yet, the Gropius House is anything but traditional New England architecture. The clapboards were installed vertically on interior walls, and for every traditional material used, Gropius introduced its mass-produced modern counterpart. His house reflects an innovative point of view in which the old became new. This, in fact, is what has been happening in New England architecture for nearly three hundred years, since the first New England housewrights combined time-honored English building forms with local materials to establish the traditional architectural vocabulary on which Gropius drew so heavily.

right and

far right

The study's double desk, designed by Marcel Breuer to Walter Gropius's specifications, allowed Gropius and his wife, Ise, to work side by side. Their innovative home, a landmark of modern design, incorporates glass block and acoustical plaster, building materials rarely used in domestic settings in the 1930s.

In 1692 in Saugus, Massachusetts, young William Boardman constructed a house that closely resembled the late-medieval architecture of seventeenth-century England. Built of massive timber framing exposed on the interior, it had a steeply pitched roof, small casement windows with diamond-shaped panes fixed by strips of lead, and a large cooking fireplace. Befitting his trade as a joiner, Boardman was skilled in cutting the massive timbers and complex joints of house frames and furniture. To ornament the interior of his own house, he hired skilled craftsmen to add chamfers and stops on the beams and molded vertical sheathing on the fireplace walls.

Boardman's house, although larger than many, had only four main rooms—a first-floor hall and a parlor with two bedchambers above—and a massive central chimney that, once heated, radiated warmth throughout the building. The front door opened into a small entry with an enclosed staircase set in front of the chimney. As was typical in seventeenth-century homes, the four rooms served multiple purposes. The hall was the family's cooking, eating, and gathering area; the parlor housed the best furniture, including two beds and bedsteads; and the upper chambers were used for sleeping and storage. Eventually the growing family needed more space, and by 1731 a new kitchen, milk room, and bedroom had been added in a line behind the chimney under a low-pitched lean-to with a sloping saltbox roof.

far right

Early-eighteenth-
century paneling
added to the Gilman
Garrison House
(1709) in Exeter, New
Hampshire, features
bold moldings, a two-
panel door, and no
mantel shelf. Classi-
cism is revealed in the
stop-fluted pilasters.

right

Like the earliest New
England houses, the
Spencer-Peirce-Little
House in Newbury,
Massachusetts, has
gables, a steeply
pitched roof, and a
center chimney.
However, its use of
stone and brick and
its great height, pro-
jecting two-story
entrance porch, and
cruciform plan make
this house unique
in New England. The
wooden extension
on the left was added
about 1800.

About the same time that the Boardmans were enjoying their enlarged house, a building of a very different style was being constructed in Newbury, Massachusetts, for Daniel Peirce Jr., a wealthy and prominent local citizen. Known today as the Spencer-Peirce-Little House, this imposing stone house has always successfully conveyed an impression of wealth and status. In the Newbury area, as in New England generally, wood was the building material of choice because of its abundance; despite the ready availability of fieldstones, masonry was rare because local limestone for mortar was scarce.

As architectural styles evolved in the years before the American Revolution, those who could afford to express their wealth and position through new houses used increasingly formal floor plans, symmetrical arrangements of both rooms and ornament, a rational system of proportion, and carefully articulated classical architectural details. Houses of this type are now referred to as Georgian because of their popularity during the reigns of the English kings George I through George IV (1714–1830).

Such houses typically had four rooms on each floor, often with two separate chimneys and a wide central hall. They were still built with massive timber frames, but now these beams were usually covered by wooden cases, the ceilings were plastered, and carefully fitted wood paneling graced the walls and doors. Larger, double-hung sash windows were used instead of hinged casements with tiny diamond-shaped panes. In addition to being commodious and comfortable homes, these houses were statements about prosperity and taste.

In 1730 in the village that is now Essex, Massachusetts, Jonathan Cogswell, a successful farmer and prominent citizen, married his second wife, Elizabeth Wade, the daughter of a wealthy mercantile family in the nearby town of Ipswich. The house to which Cogswell brought his new bride, later known as Cogswell's Grant, had been expanded two years earlier from a seventeenth-century house belonging to his father. The expanded house included a new kitchen, a broad stair hall, and three stylish rooms. The new rooms reflected the new Georgian architectural ideas, but like other early Georgian houses they still showed traces of their earlier roots in the large kitchen fireplace with the oven at the rear and in the cased beams extending below the plaster ceiling and projecting into the corners of the rooms. The Cogswells' two new front rooms, one on each floor, have paneled chimney walls with bold moldings, molded door frames, and paneled doors. Both these rooms show evidence of eighteenth-century ornamental painting that was replicated when the house was restored; the chamber above has cedar graining and green-painted

The ordered appearance of Cogswell's Grant in Essex, Massachusetts, is somewhat deceptive. The oldest portions are the rooms at the left and the broad interior stair hall, built attached to an existing seventeenth-century house that was later torn down and replaced by the rooms on the right. Behind the house are barns dating from the eighteenth and nineteenth centuries.

woodwork, while the sitting room below has richly textured green paneling. Later in the century the Cogswells replaced the oldest part of the house with four more rooms that adjoined those built in 1728.

As the Georgian style grew in popularity throughout New England, homeowners and builders relied heavily on the proportions, designs, plans, structural schemes, and decorative details found in English architectural pattern books, such as Abraham Swan's *British Architect*, first published in 1745, and William Pain's *Builder's Companion*, published in 1758. These books served as direct sources or as inspirations for house plans and architectural ornament inside and outside houses up and down the New England seacoast in the last half of the eighteenth century. Their use reflects a broader understanding of architecture among educated people as well as increasing prosperity, which allowed for the use of expensive materials and nonfunctional details that were time consuming to produce.

Col. Josiah Quincy was clearly influenced by English architectural styles when he constructed his new two-and-one-half-story Georgian home in Quincy, Massachusetts, in 1770. After a faulty oven repair caused his earlier house to burn to the ground, Quincy saw an opportunity to build in the latest taste. Only thirteen days after the fire, Quincy invited the Dorchester housewright Edward Pierce to what would now be called a business dinner. The food must have been good and the conversation productive, for Quincy engaged Pierce to provide a plan for his new house, which when completed handsomely displayed the full range of Georgian details. The window panes, ten by fourteen inches, in particular "excited the admiration and curiosity of the neighborhood." The classical perfection of the Quincy House led to its preservation, almost unchanged, through five generations of a family whose increasing wealth and social prominence could easily have tempted them to make radical changes.

left

A classic example of Georgian architecture, the Quincy House in Quincy, Massachusetts, boasts an innovative monitor roof, one of the earliest surviving examples in New England. Used for conducting household tasks and housing servants or guests, the rooms under the roof were warmed by small fireplaces in winter and cooled by open windows in summer.

Nearly one hundred miles north of Quincy lie the towns of Exeter and Portsmouth, New Hampshire, linked by tidal rivers to towns such as South Berwick, Maine. Throughout this region the ideals of Georgian architecture and design were translated from English pattern books by a skilled group of local joiners, carvers, and cabinetmakers, including Michael Whidden, Ebenezer Dearing, Richard Mills, their sons, and others. They worked in many communities, traveling easily by water from town to town. An exceptional example of their work is the elegant 1774 Georgian house in South Berwick built for John Haggins and later the home of the author Sarah Orne Jewett, who wrote some of her most important works there. In nearby Portsmouth, New Hampshire, in 1784, John Langdon, a wealthy merchant who later became governor, commissioned woodworkers from the same skilled group to build an even larger house in the imposing Georgian style. Behind its well-proportioned facade and prominent portico, the interiors are ornamented with gracefully carved rococo woodwork based on forty-year-old English designs.

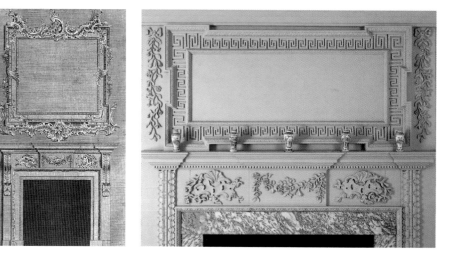

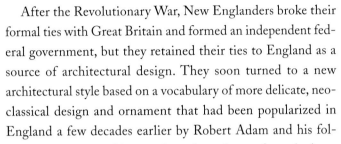

After the Revolutionary War, New Englanders broke their formal ties with Great Britain and formed an independent federal government, but they retained their ties to England as a source of architectural design. They soon turned to a new architectural style based on a vocabulary of more delicate, neo-classical design and ornament that had been popularized in England a few decades earlier by Robert Adam and his followers. Designs in this taste brought a change from the heavy moldings and occasional rococo carving of the Georgian period. In the Federal period a new profession developed—that of the architect.

New England's first professional architect was Charles Bulfinch, best known today as the designer of the Massachusetts State House (1795–97). Bulfinch traveled in England just after the war and familiarized himself with the Adamesque style, characterized by delicate ornamentation and the use of classical architectural elements modeled on those found in the buried cities of Pompeii and Herculaneum during the excavations begun in 1753. Simplifying this new style, Bulfinch designed several of the new nation's public buildings, later including the rotunda of the U.S. Capitol, and houses for some of Boston's most prominent citizens.

Among them were his friend Harrison Gray Otis, a young lawyer and politician, and Otis's wealthy wife, Sally, who in 1795 commissioned Bulfinch to design an elegant house at the foot of Beacon Hill—a three-story brick town house with seventeen rooms and Federal-style detailing, today the only freestanding late-eighteenth-century house remaining in Boston. Although the house, completed in 1796, was sold by the Otises in 1801 and later used as a boardinghouse, most of the original architectural details, including samples of many of the original wallpapers, have survived. Today the restored Otis House serves as the headquarters of Historic New England.

above

Federal details of the Otis House in Boston include an elliptical fanlight over the front door, a lunette on the third floor, six-paned double-hung windows, and slender end chimneys delineating a center hall.

left

The wallpaper pattern in the parlor chamber is a reproduction of one chosen by the Otises when the house was built.

right

The Nickels-Sortwell House in Wiscasset, Maine—with its elegant facade, imposing scale, and elaborate ornamentation—reflects the prosperity and sophistication of the shipbuilding and maritime trade era.

Bulfinch's work was admired by many, including Asher Benjamin, a young architect who published America's first pattern book, *The Country Builder's Assistant*, in 1797, while working in Greenfield, in western Massachusetts. In 1803 Benjamin moved to Boston, where he designed the West Church, which was built next door to the Otis House in 1806. Through his many publications, Benjamin helped spread Bulfinch's interpretation of the Federal style to more rural areas of New England.

The strong influence of such publications is easily seen in the small coastal community of Wiscasset, Maine, where Capt. William Nickels built a handsome three-story house in 1807. The entrance doorway was copied by a local craftsman directly from plate 30 of Benjamin's 1806 book, *The American Builder's Companion*, which incorporated both Benjamin's own design ideas and some of Bulfinch's. The main portion of the house is symmetrical, with a room on either side of the central stair hall on the first two floors and two rooms on either side on the third floor. The impressive cantilevered oval staircase extends from the first to the third floor and is lighted by a conical skylight in the domed ceiling of the hallway. This sophisticated feature was also illustrated in English architectural design books, indicating that Nickels and his builder were influenced not only by American patterns but also perhaps by William Pain's 1796 English pattern book, *The Practical House Carpenter*.

opposite

Light floods through the elaborate fanlight and sidelights into the stair hall of the Nickels-Sortwell House. The gracefully curving stair leads to two large chambers on the second floor and four on the third.

An important representation of local vernacular architecture, the Marrett House in Standish, Maine, is a classic late-eighteenth-century homestead with well-preserved additions and alterations from the mid-nineteenth century.

Following President Thomas Jefferson's Embargo Act of 1807, which prohibited foreign trade, and the War of 1812, New England's thriving seaports became less active, and fortunes were lost. Despite the subsequent growth of textile manufacturing in New England, lack of money slowed the pace of architectural development. Simple vernacular buildings continued to be built in the region throughout the nineteenth century, but during the 1830s and 1840s architects and builders began to copy historical forms and ornament in more exact ways, resulting in a picturesque aesthetic influenced by Greek and then Gothic and Italianate styles. These revival styles, which followed in close order and even overlapped in their popularity, can be found in fully developed form in New England, but pure examples are far outnumbered by ver-

nacular house forms embellished with ornament in one of the popular revival styles.

For many who were concerned with creating a fashionable architectural statement, building a new house was not essential. One of the most prominent residences in Standish, Maine, has always been the Reverend Daniel Marrett's 1789 house, with its central chimney and tight staircase in the entry. In 1840, however, the minister's son, Avery, updated the old house by raising the roof to accommodate a stylish new cornice, adding ornamental window caps and handsome pilasters at the corners of the house, and introducing some new interior woodwork in the Greek Revival style. He also added a side porch with classical columns and built an ell, perpendicular to the main house, that connected with a large new barn.

The Bowen House in Woodstock, Connecticut, is one of the finest and most complete examples of Gothic Revival architecture in America. Even its outbuildings, including the barn and icehouse, are all richly ornamented with Gothic detail. Long known as Roseland Cottage, the exterior of the whole complex was painted this shade of pink in the 1880s.

Only a few years after the Marretts updated their Georgian house, Henry Chandler Bowen undertook a much more ambitious project in his hometown of Woodstock, Connecticut. His 1846 Roseland Cottage, built wholly in the newly fashionable Gothic Revival style, has an asymmetrical plan, towering terra-cotta chimney pots, an oriel window, and a full range of outbuildings with Gothic ornament. With its stained glass, steep crocketed gables, and vertical board-and-batten siding pointing heavenward—all features incorporating uplifting moral and religious associations—Bowen's house stands in bold contrast to its Federal-style neighbors surrounding the town common. It is at once an expression of moral virtue and of Bowen's financial success, the fashionable New York world of which he had become a part, and his desire to make a statement in his native community.

In *The Architecture of Country Houses* (1850), Andrew Jackson Downing may well have been describing Bowen when he wrote of "men of imagination—men whose aspirations never leave them at rest—men whose ambition and energy will give them no peace within the mere bounds of rationality":

These are the men for picturesque villas—country houses with high roofs, steep gables, unsymmetrical and capricious forms. It is for such that the architect may safely introduce the tower and the campanile—and any and every feature that indicates originality, boldness, energy, and variety of character. To find a really original man living in an original and characteristic house, is as satisfactory as to find an eagle's nest built on the top of a mountain crag.

right

Joseph Collins Wells, the architect of Roseland Cottage, may have painted this charming watercolor at the time the house was built. For his design Wells received $500, a commission of five percent of the total construction cost of $10,000.

Although some men like Bowen dared to express themselves in bold new architectural forms, many New Englanders clung to tradition. Whether for the power of familiar association or just lack of money, traditional foursquare house plans with minimal architectural ornament continued to be used for more than a century. Sometimes one room was updated in a new style while others were left unchanged. Sometimes accurately reproduced details from many historical periods were blended together willy-nilly in a completely ahistorical pattern.

At John Langdon's house in Portsmouth, New Hampshire, the Georgian facade and the primary interiors changed little throughout the nineteenth century, but sometime after 1836, following a small fire, the back parlor was remodeled in the Greek Revival style and a bay window added. In 1905–6 the owners—Woodbury Langdon, a descendant and namesake of John Langdon's brother, and his wife, Elizabeth, also a John Langdon descendant—hired the noted architecture firm McKim,

To preserve a link with the past, Elizabeth Langdon wanted her new dining room to be octagonal like the one in Woodbury Langdon's 1785 brick house in Portsmouth. While not strictly an octagon, it recalls the earlier room in both its architecture and its furniture.

Mead, and White to replace the original kitchen and service ell with a new wing containing a dining room, a kitchen, a pantry, and servants' rooms. The massive dining room, the addition's most striking feature, incorporated woodwork made by the Boston firm Irving and Casson and based on Federal-period details in the dining room of Woodbury Langdon's first Portsmouth house, built about 1785. This house had been nearly destroyed in a disastrous fire in September 1884, but the dining room was saved and installed in the town's Rockingham Hotel, then just being built. For the Langdons, the association of these designs with an ancestor was as important as the opportunity to entertain on a grand scale in this magnificent new room.

This blending of late Georgian building forms and reproduced Federal detail is typical of early-twentieth-century work done in a style intended to be historical and today known as Colonial Revival. Indeed, these basic vernacular forms and details are often adopted and enhanced by builders even today. Both are incorporated in the postmodern style by both skilled designers and ambitious consumers and make traditional New England architecture familiar to everyone.

Regardless of their chosen style or richness of ornament, all these buildings were created to shelter families as well as express the taste and status of their owners. Within their walls, New England families pursued their daily work, prepared and ate their meals, entertained their friends, gave birth, and died. From the local joiner William Boardman to the internationally renowned architect Walter Gropius, the purpose of the house remained the same.

left

The mid-nineteenth-century bay window became an integrated part of the Langdon House, as did the wing designed by McKim, Mead, and White fifty years later to house the dining room, pantry, kitchen, and servants' quarters.

ROOMS OF THEIR OWN

"I like to think of young Tristram [Coffin] as he plied his trade or took up his many civic burdens in this house of his.... There was one room on the ground floor, one room on the second floor, perhaps two, and an attic. Young couples today start housekeeping in a kitchenette apartment, with parlor, bed room, bath and kitchenette. Tristram's parlor and kitchen were one and the same, and the bath was eliminated."

James W. Spring, "The Coffin House in Newbury, Massachusetts and Those Who Have Made It Their Home," *Old-Time New England*, July 1929

Most early New Englanders like Tristram Coffin Jr. lived in one or two multipurpose rooms, with nothing to separate areas used for different activities. Dirty, smoky, smelly, and wet work was undertaken in the same rooms used for sleeping, eating, and entertaining, sometimes all simultaneously. Windows, if any, were small casements, so interiors were often dark and stuffy. The heat generated by a fire for cooking or heating water could be almost unbearable in the summer, although in wintertime snow might drift in around the windows in the same room and never melt. Several generations—older parents, newlyweds, and young families—often lived together in these crowded quarters. As prosperity increased for some people, standards of living improved and brought more orderly interiors, a distinction between spaces for private and public activities, and more comfortable and stylish furnishings.

The two-story house built by Judith and Tristram Coffin Jr. in 1678, across the road from the meeting house, had a single room on each floor, each with a fireplace and two casement windows. Here the Coffins lived out their lives with four of their fourteen children, along with young relatives, apprentices, and hired hands. Here food was cooked and eaten, clothes were sewn and laundered, town business was discussed at the great table next to the fire, and Judith and Tristram were nursed at the end of their long lives.

An inventory of the household furnishings taken after Tristram's death makes it clear that the few beds and chests were shared by many family members. People sat on chairs, benches, storage chests, beds, upturned barrels and buckets, and the floor. Family members must have eaten from a common plate or dish with spoons or their fingers; there were no forks and only a few pewter plates. Light from a single candlestick was augmented by firelight, but the rooms were never very bright. Despite the house's apparent confusion and obvious discomfort, the Coffin family was highly regarded in the Newbury community. A tailor and farmer, Tristram served as a selectman, church deacon, and member of the town militia. To his house came town officers, church members, and close neighbors to meet, work, talk, and pray. All lived in similar or even smaller houses.

By the time Tristram and Judith's youngest son, Nathaniel, was married in 1693, his sisters had married and moved out and his brothers had received some land on which to establish their own households. Nathaniel and his wife moved into the two-room house with his parents, then in their sixties. By 1712 new rooms were constructed on the back side of the original chimney; a generation later this section, too, was enlarged with additional rooms. By the mid-eighteenth century the house sheltered thirteen people representing three generations. How the space was divided among these three households is unclear, but ownership and control rested with the patriarch.

The growth of the Coffin House was organic, not planned. The extended family added a few rooms at a time, reallocated space in response to the changing number of occupants, and added fireplaces and created larger windows for greater comfort. Not until about 1815, when the Coffins set aside a room as a parlor and decorated it with wallpaper, did they use their house and furnishings as an explicit statement of their comfortable prosperity and long-standing status as church and community leaders.

The evolution of the Coffin family's house and their expanding financial resources was by no means unique among colonial New England families. For nearly thirty years Jonathan Sayward, a successful merchant in York Harbor, Maine, made few changes to the twenty-year-old house he inherited from his father in 1735. In the 1760s Sayward, by then financially comfortable, hired a local craftsman named Samuel Sewall to make a high chest of drawers and add new molded cornices in the sitting room, ordered a set of side chairs in the Chippendale style from a Boston cabinet-maker, commissioned Joseph Blackburn to paint a large portrait of his beautiful daughter, Sally, his only child, and bought wallpaper for the best parlor, where the chairs were placed and the portraits hung.

Before he died in 1797, Sayward prepared a will—drawn up, signed, witnessed, and approved by the probate judge—in which he bequeathed his "homestead, with the buildings of every kind thereon, and appurtenance there unto belonging" to Sally's eldest son, Jonathan Sayward Barrell. (Sally and her husband were already comfortably settled on a nearby farm, so the homestead passed to the next generation.) Sayward also specified that his second wife, Elizabeth, was to continue living in the house and carefully designated the division of living quarters, leaving to her the northwest end of the "dwelling house from the Garret to the Cellar, inclusively and authority to open a passageway from the West Room thro' the bed room to the Kitchen, if she pleases." Elizabeth also had the right to use a cane chair and two leather chairs, reupholster the "Easy Chair," and sit in the "pew where she usually sits on the Sabbath." Barrell was to provide her with "five cords of Hard Wood, and five Cords of hemlock, or Pine, to be delivered annually at the house," and they were to share the kitchen, garden, and family carriage, a horse-drawn chaise.

far left

One of the spaces Jonathan Sayward set aside for the use of his second wife, Elizabeth, during her widowhood was the house's west room. Joseph Blackburn's portrait of Sayward's daughter, Sally, remains where it has been since it was hung in the Sayward family's York Harbor, Maine, home in 1761.

left

In 1770, records show, Jonathan Sayward purchased some blue-checked linen, which may have been made into bed curtains for the first-floor bedroom (left). The parlor chamber is simply furnished with an imported looking glass and a locally made chest of drawers (right).

At the time this watercolor of the Sayward-Wheeler House was painted, in the 1880s, the house was occupied by Jonathan Sayward's great-granddaughters Elizabeth and Mary Barrell.

far right

In the tiny entry of the Sayward-Wheeler House, the staircase makes three turns against the chimney. Some of Jonathan Sayward's furniture is still in place.

Realizing that sharing living space might be awkward, Sayward offered his widow the opportunity to make a separate entrance from the kitchen into her portion of the house, and she did so. She did not, however, create a doorway between her first-floor chamber and the front parlor, even though she could pass from one to the other only by going through the sitting room of her step-grandson's family, by going out the kitchen door and around the house and then entering the front door, or by going up the back stairs and down the front.

Sayward's provisions regarding the use of rooms are very specific, but whether they were actually followed is not known. Jonathan Sayward Barrell and his step-grandmother may have lived together in harmony, changing their use of the various rooms according to the seasons or some other circumstance. Although the parlor belonged to Elizabeth, the whole family may have assembled there on occasion, as when, for example, the minister came to call. On the other hand, the inconvenience of Elizabeth's access to the parlor may have meant that neither she nor anyone else used it daily. Or perhaps the use of rooms was a source of tension and dispute.

Jonathan Sayward was not alone in designating a grandson as his heir. After Josiah Quincy Jr. died at sea in 1775, his father, Col. Josiah Quincy, drew up a will in which he left his new large house and all its furnishings to his grandson Josiah III. The Quincy House, which twelve-year-old Josiah III inherited in 1784, must have looked like many of the other imposing New England houses built and furnished in the years immediately before the American Revolution: a large building designed with Georgian detail, a broad central hallway, and ample rooms with fireplaces occasionally ornamented with imported tiles and decorated with strong colors, bold wallpaper designs, and solid mahogany or walnut Chippendale furniture. In many rooms the color of the curtains, upholstery and wallpaper was the same; primary colors, such as red, were preferred, as at the Sarah Orne Jewett House in South Berwick, Maine.

In sharp contrast to the unpretentious improvements made in the Coffin and Sayward Houses and the bold Georgian interiors of the Quincy and Jewett Houses were the impressive new houses built and furnished after the Revolution by the elite in thriving coastal cities. Acutely aware of architectural styles and fashionable furnishings, men such as John Langdon, Harrison Gray Otis, and James Rundlet demanded large houses that expressed their prosperity and provided an appropriate level of comfort. They ordered fashionable goods from London, patronized local merchants, and commissioned cabinetmakers to provide stylish, specialized pieces including dining tables, sideboards, and washstands. Industrial production of ceramics and textiles in England and their increasing availability made possible whole sets of ceramic dinnerware and a much more liberal use of colorful wallpaper, textiles for window and bed curtains, and upholstered furniture. Families with an improving standard of cleanliness and a high regard for genteel behavior demanded an abundance of bed and table linen, highly specialized furnishings, more secluded privies, and, not least, diligent servants.

above

In Josiah Quincy's home in Quincy, Massachusetts, a japanned high chest, acquired in 1740, has survived two fires.

left

Eighteenth-century English flocked red-on-pink wallpaper in the parlor chamber at the Sarah Orne Jewett House in South Berwick, Maine, reflects contemporary tastes for strong colors.

When John Langdon engaged local craftsmen to construct his handsome new house in Portsmouth, New Hampshire, in 1784, his intention was to create an impressive space in which to entertain. Only one other house in a forty-mile radius had a double drawing room on this scale, and none had so much exuberant rococo carving. The first guests invited to see this room must have marveled at the furnishings that Langdon had ordered from London: a "Wilton or other Carpet, Newest fashion," four "Window Curtains completely made of purple and white furniture [fabric], or any other color that will be most suitable for the Room which is paper'd with a plain pink paper," four cushions for the window seats, and a "pair of large Handsome Looking Glasses, one for each end of the room." This ensemble was completed with twelve "Large Arm'd Chairs" and a settee, the backs and seats of which were covered in the same purple-and-white fabric as the window curtains and cushions.

For all this lavish display, Langdon's new house was an old-fashioned place. Its most impressive architectural ornament was the rococo carving, based on a forty-year-old design. Neither architecture nor furnishings reflected the neoclassical taste that was already being seen in Philadelphia, New York, and Boston. Langdon was forty-five years old when he began furnishing his new house, and his taste had clearly been formed in his youth. His house was furnished with quality goods intended to last a lifetime and expressed the New Englander's desire for things that were useful but tasteful, rich but not gaudy.

above

A delegate to the Second Continental Congress in 1775–76, John Langdon later served as senator from New Hampshire and then as governor. Edward Savage is believed to have painted this portrait around 1790.

right

In the entry hall of the Governor John Langdon House in Portsmouth, New Hampshire, each staircase step features three turning patterns. The newel post, balusters, and paneling are probably by Ebenezer Clifford.

Furnishings in the latest taste filled the first home of the young Boston lawyer Harrison Gray Otis and his wife, the beautiful and accomplished Sally Foster, whom he married in 1790. William Foster had provided his daughter with a generous marriage portion: linen, muslin, and silk; a dining service that included "Table Set China," a "Silver Tea Pott, Cream Pail and Spoon, 8 large Spoons and 12 Tea Spoons," and "2 pair Plated Candlesticks"; beds, tables, chairs, and carpets; and fireplace and cooking equipment.

In 1793 Otis purchased a lot on Cambridge Street and began conversations with a young friend, the architect Charles Bulfinch, about the plan of a new house. The "Large new house" had seventeen rooms and featured both a parlor and a dining room on the first floor and a grand withdrawing room for entertaining on the second floor. The wide front hallway with its formal staircase, much more delicate than those found in earlier Georgian houses, was the space in which the host and hostess and their guests moved between the dining room and the parlor and ascended to the more elegant withdrawing room. The enclosed rear stairway, reflecting new standards of gentility, made it possible for servants to move undetected as their work took them from the kitchen to the public and private spaces on the first and second floors and to the third floor, carrying up food, beverages, water, firewood, new candles, clean clothing, brooms, housecleaning materials, and fresh bed linens and bringing down soiled bed linens and dirty clothing, dirty water, full chamber pots, dirty dishes, and buckets of ashes, food scraps, and candle stubs. Undoubtedly, the children clambered up and down both staircases, blurring the social differentiation intended by the architect and sought by their parents.

left

**The parlor of the
Harrison Gray Otis
House in Boston
features a plain
yellow paper with a
block-printed border
in the "Etruscan"
style, which enjoyed
a brief popularity in
America in the 1790s.**

below

**The Otis House's
entrance hall was a
place of public
parade. New to the
Federal period are the
fanlights and side-
lights around the door
and the second-story
window and the
display of many
pictures on the walls.**

left

On James Rundlet's death in 1852, his obituary described his house in Portsmouth, New Hampshire, as "imposing in appearance and an object of envy to many who predicted with wise nods that so much pride must have a fall and concluded that he had built his house too high—but they happen to have been mistaken."

During the prosperous years immediately preceding Jefferson's embargo of 1807 and the War of 1812, many New England merchants and sea captains in smaller cities outside Boston were able to build large houses in the new Federal style. James Rundlet in Portsmouth, New Hampshire, hired local craftsmen to give his family one of the most grand. Completed in 1808, the house incorporated new cooking and heating technology and was furnished with English wallpaper, glassware, and ceramics as well as the products of Portsmouth's celebrated cabinetmaker Langley Boardman and his contemporaries. Here, too, public and private spaces were sharply differentiated; the enclosed service stairs shielded much of the indoor activity from public view, the privy was indoors (in the attached ell), and the service yard was separate from the garden.

far left

In September 1809 James and Jane Rundlet's new parlor was papered with a "Peach Damask" pattern and a "Paris Flock" border. The original wallpaper remains in place.

The adjoining double parlors at Roseland Cottage in Wood-stock, Connecticut, still contain black walnut chairs from the original Gothic furnishings of 1846 as well as carved rose-wood rococo revival-style chairs from the family's winter home in Brooklyn, New York. The stained-glass windows are part of the original decorative scheme, while the Lincrusta-Walton wall covering was installed fifty years later.

Unlike Langdon, Otis, and Rundlet, Richard Tucker Jr., a Wiscasset, Maine, merchant, did not build a new house for his young bride, Mollie Armstrong, when they married in 1857, nor did her father provide their furnishings. Instead, the next year Tucker purchased a handsome fifty-year-old hilltop house and traveled to Boston to purchase furniture, leaving seventeen-year-old Mollie at home with their infant daughter. She must have had great confidence in her husband's taste and understanding of what would be needed, for she wrote to him, "I don't bother myself at all about the furniture, I know you love pretty things as well as I do and that your taste and judgment are faultless. I know you will do right."

Tucker's purchases were sent by ship from Boston directly to Wiscasset, and he was soon billed for the costs of carting fourteen loads of furniture from the docks on the Sheepscot River up the hill to the newly remodeled house, later known as Castle Tucker. Bills from Boston dealers reveal that the loads included a walnut parlor set, a "fancy grand piano with cover," a marble-top center table, a mirror to be hung over the mantel, a hat tree, four complete bedroom sets, a crib, and six sets of curtains and valances. Tucker owned a copy of the 1856 edition of Downing's *Architecture of Country Houses,* and it seems likely that he took it to Boston with him on his buying trip, for many of the furnishings he purchased are similar to those recommended by Downing.

After the family had lived in the house for several long cold winters, Tucker added a south-facing wing adjacent to the kitchen that included a new dining room in the Elizabethan style advocated by Downing. Sandwiched between the warm kitchen and the sunshine, this low-ceilinged room was much warmer than the old dining room. Tucker's father commented approvingly that Richard's "fixings are made in good taste . . . plain, neat, and by no means gaudy and extravagant."

At Castle Tucker in Wiscasset, Maine, the parlor set "in good modern, comfortable style" ordered in Boston by Richard Tucker in 1858 still stands on the carpet he ordered at the same time. New wall-paper and curtains replaced the originals later in the century.

right

Redesigned by John Hubbard Sturgis in 1862, the billiard room of the Codman House in Lincoln, Massachusetts, was apparently seldom used. In a letter home, Ogden Codman Jr. disparaged "that dreadful Billiard table [which] has always been an eyesore and a stumbling block."

above

In 1897, at Ogden Jr.'s urging, the billiard room—"the nicest room of all"—was refurnished as a library to make it "comfortable and nice," as he wanted.

Just a few years later, in 1862, Ogden Codman Sr. and his wife, Sarah Fletcher Bradlee Codman, also purchased an old house after one year of marriage spent living with parents. Their twelve-room, three-story house in Lincoln, Massachusetts, had once belonged to Ogden's grandfather, John Codman. Intending to live there year-round, Ogden engaged his brother-in-law John Hubbard Sturgis to make architectural changes, adding porches and redesigning elements of the entrance hall, billiard room, and dining room. For their furnishings the Codmans sought the advice of the noted decorator Leon Marcotte in New York City, believing that he could provide a more integrated selection of imported articles than Boston offered. On November 21, 1862, they received Marcotte's proposals for furniture, carpeting, wallpaper, curtains, and upholstery fabric; orders were soon sent for these items and additional pieces.

above

The Codman House dining room features 1860s woodwork and Elizabethan ceiling designed by Sturgis. The "Butternut and black dining extension table," swan's-head chairs, and low sideboard were ordered from Leon Marcotte in New York.

The next generation of the Codman family did not fully appreciate the stylish Victorian interiors created in the 1860s. In 1897, after making careful architectural drawings of many details of the house, Ogden Jr., a practicing architect and coauthor with Edith Wharton of *The Decoration of Houses* (1897), restored the eighteenth-century paneling and redecorated several rooms. Thirty years later he complained to his brother Tom:

I wish he [Sturgis] had the sense not to try to bring the house 'up to date' but had been satisfied [with] just leaving the design alone. . . . I am sure the old simple colonial paneling and wainscoting was much nicer really than what he and Marcotte did to the billiard room, and dining room, and those dreadful mantels he designed for the bedrooms. But I suppose that in 1862 no one thought anything old fashioned was nice at all. Perhaps if he had left everything as it was I should never have been inspired with passion for putting things back as they were. But that has been a great pleasure to me.

far left

The paneled room at the Codman House retains the original paneling from about 1740, painted white since the house's renovation by Ogden Codman Sr. in the 1860s. The French taste in furnishings and fabrics reflects his son's influence thirty years later.

left

After the Codman family returned from living in France in 1884, the paneled room's window cornices, curtains, carpets, and some of the furniture ordered from Marcotte were still in use. The room stayed this way until Ogden Jr. redecorated it in the 1890s.

far right

The writer Sarah Orne Jewett's own bedroom in the Jewett House in South Berwick, Maine, remains as she left it, "with the chairs all in their places." The landscape painting is by a friend, the Boston artist Sarah Wyman Whitman.

Similar pleasure in "putting things back as they were" was enjoyed by Emily Tyson and her stepdaughter, Elise, when they were inspired by Sarah Orne Jewett to purchase the old Hamilton House in South Berwick, Maine, in 1898. Their changes to the house reflected their desire for convenient summer living and their respect for the handsome Georgian design. With the help of the Boston architect Herbert Browne, they added functional spaces—a porch and kitchen wing to the east and a sleeping porch and piazza to the west—while respecting the house's original fabric and limiting structural changes to relocating a back stairway in order to enlarge the dining room.

The role of the house in a family's life evolved as New England grew and changed. In the mid-seventeenth century, when the Coffins built their house, the family's most basic need—shelter—was the primary concern. Later, Jonathan Sayward sought to make his home more comfortable and stylish but remained conservative in his approach. By the time New England prospered, wealthy men like John Langdon, Harry Otis, and James Rundlet were expressing their places in society through grand, new homes. As New Englanders celebrated the country's centennial and looked toward the twentieth century, the Codmans, Tysons, and many others attempted to bring older houses back to a romanticized vision of the past. Despite these changes over time, the home remained central to each family's life and sense of itself.

right

The ribbon windows on the second floor of the Gropius House in Lincoln, Massachusetts, were designed to carefully frame the landscape, bring in abundant natural light, and afford privacy for the family.

At the Boston home where they lived for twenty-eight years before moving to The Vale in Waltham, Massachusetts, Arthur and Ella Lyman employed a teacher to instruct their son Ronald (second from right) and three children of friends in the house's third-floor nursery.

right

Toys belonging to the Codman children, still at their home in Lincoln, Massachusetts, include "Winter Amusements," "A Fortress to Build," a theater "for the Use and Entertainment of Children in Their Leisure Hours," and much-loved dolls.

far right

Death was an ever-present fact for New England families. Like others, the Goodwins, the owners of the Hamilton House in South Berwick, Maine, in the late nineteenth century, maintained their own cemetery on their land.

New England households long extended far beyond the nuclear family considered normal today. Those who lived together—parents and children, widows and widowers, maiden aunts and crotchety uncles, orphaned cousins, devoted nursemaids, homesick hired girls, and temperamental cooks—were often active parts of the household, whether they were related to each other or not. Their lives together may have been cut short by tragic accidents or sudden illness, hampered by birth defects, or cruelly altered by chronic disease, alcoholism, mental instability, or the infirmities of old age. Family members were dependent on one another for the necessities and comforts of everyday life, and they were bound by the structures of work and social ritual, the obligation of support, and the bonds of caring.

TIES THAT BIND

"The nursery costs me more to leave than any other room of the house, for I have the most happy and tender associations with it, and I can never have little children again."

Ella Lowell Lyman, diary, 1886

At the Boston home where they lived for twenty-eight years before moving to The Vale in Waltham, Massachusetts, Arthur and Ella Lyman employed a teacher to instruct their son Ronald (second from right) and three children of friends in the house's third-floor nursery.

right

Toys belonging to the Codman children, still at their home in Lincoln, Massachusetts, include "Winter Amusements," "A Fortress to Build," a theater "for the Use and Entertainment of Children in Their Leisure Hours," and much-loved dolls.

far right

Death was an everpresent fact for New England families. Like others, the Goodwins, the owners of the Hamilton House in South Berwick, Maine, in the late nineteenth century, maintained their own cemetery on their land.

New England households long extended far beyond the nuclear family considered normal today. Those who lived together—parents and children, widows and widowers, maiden aunts and crotchety uncles, orphaned cousins, devoted nursemaids, homesick hired girls, and temperamental cooks—were often active parts of the household, whether they were related to each other or not. Their lives together may have been cut short by tragic accidents or sudden illness, hampered by birth defects, or cruelly altered by chronic disease, alcoholism, mental instability, or the infirmities of old age. Family members were dependent on one another for the necessities and comforts of everyday life, and they were bound by the structures of work and social ritual, the obligation of support, and the bonds of caring.

Colonial New England families often relied on some outside help for domestic chores. Many, even those of moderate means, hired girls or women who lived in and assisted with routine chores such as cooking, scrubbing, spinning, and laundry. Wealthy urban families had, in addition, serving men, butlers, and coachmen, some of whom wore livery or uniforms (women servants had no such mark of distinction). A small percentage of the wealthiest New Englanders owned slaves, most of whom worked as indoor servants or coachmen.

Jonathan Sayward owned at least two slaves: Cato, who ran away once in 1769 and was sold in 1781 for $285, and Prince Sayward, who served for forty years before "the new constitution [of 1789] made him free." Perhaps in gratitude for this long service or perhaps because of their close companionship over forty years, Sayward paid the expenses of Prince's last illness and burial a few months later.

In their large household in nearby Portsmouth, New Hampshire, John and Elizabeth Langdon relied for help on servants, at least some of whom slept in rooms on the third floor on the "good strong cheap Beds, Bedding & Bedsteads without Posts or Curtains for Servant Men & Maids" that Langdon had ordered from London in 1766. Among the twenty contracts between John Langdon and servants, none is with women, suggesting that the employment of women servants was less structured. In a 1789 contract with Charles Herenton, typical of the day, he agreed "with John Langdon, Esq. To live with him for 12 months in the Capacity of a Servant, to drive the Carriage as Coachman, take care of horses, Tend at Table, or any Business about the house whatever." These servants were paid $4 to $12 per month, about half the rate of pay of unskilled day labor in the town.

At least one of Langdon's menservants, Siras (or Cyrus) Bruce, appears to have been an illiterate slave who was freed sometime before 1783, when he signed with his mark a contract to work "as a domestic servant in any sort of business the said Langdon may require for a term of twelve months." Outfitted with a handsome livery with metal buttons and white breeches, he continued to work for Langdon in his grand new house as late as 1797, living rent free nearby in a small house owned by Langdon. It may have been Siras who opened the door when Gen. George Washington arrived to dine and take "tea with a large circle of ladies" at Langdon's house on Monday November 2, 1789.

left

The elaborately carved parlor of the Governor John Langdon House in Portsmouth, New Hampshire, may have inspired George Washington's observation in his diary that "[t]here are some good houses [here] (among which Col. Langdon's may be esteemed the first)."

In Boston, Sally and Harrison Gray Otis, who had begun his career as a lawyer involved in real estate development and eventually became one of the wealthiest men in the city, required much help with their large family. They employed a manservant to drive carriages, care for horses, and wait on table and also hired women as nurse-maids, housemaids, cooks, and laundresses, many of whom lived in. Otis also served as a delegate to Congress, attending annual sessions in Philadelphia until 1800 and one in Washington the following year. He was a devoted husband, often writing several times a week and frequently expressing his wish that they could share a pillow. In November 1797, during Sally's seventh pregnancy, he urged her to move into the warmer withdrawing room if the bedchamber chimney could not be fixed. Subsequent letters reveal that she was despondent and fearful about the baby's delivery, perhaps because her son George, born early in 1797, had died soon after birth. Otis insisted that his wife not nurse the new baby; anticipating the "little stranger crying by your side on the Pallett," he wrote, "You will not however allow yourself to be troubled by it, but keep yourself calm and quiet and give it to its nurse." Sally gave birth to Sophia Harrison Otis on March 29, 1798. The news of her being "safe abed" after being "ill only for three hours" reached Harry in Philadelphia on April 3.

Whether from illness, accident, premature birth, choking, burns, or unknown causes, many families faced the death of at least one young child. The Otises lost both George and Mary in infancy, and in July 1806 their son Allyne, then ten years old, drowned while swimming in the Charles River. Like many of their contemporaries, the Otises named their next son, born thirteen months later, for the deceased one, and in 1810 they named their last son George, thus perpetuating the memory of the infant they had lost thirteen years earlier.

right

Harry and Sally Otis shared a loving marriage of forty-six years that endured through the births of eleven children and the deaths of three. "I always knew that my habits were naturally domestic and that my happiness was to be formed only in the bosom of my family," he wrote her on December 3, 1797.

Other families coped with death in their own ways. The late-eighteenth-century fascination with science and the New Englander's devotion to religion coincided at the Spencer-Peirce-Little Farm in Newbury, Massachusetts, in March 1808, when Offin Boardman chronicled the illness and death of his young grandson. On Tuesday, March 22, the child, who was visiting Boardman, suddenly became ill, and by four o'clock "Lettel Dear Offin" was in the "Aganeys of Death." While the boy struggled to breathe, five doctors were called in, trying to determine whether the problem was "a sead Swolard [seed swallowed] in the wind pipe" or an infection, "the Quinsey." The child continued in "a Distressin Sitwashon" and great pain for five days, gradually weakening while his anguished family prayed that he be either "raised to health for A Comfort to his parents" or "Releved from pain & have an Essey Death & Rest in the Arms of his Blessed Jesus Christ." On Monday, March 28, "at 9 Am the Dear Littel Offin Departed this Life." Three hours later the child "was Opend & [they] fownd the oring [orange] Seed in the bottom of the Wind pipe which was the Cause of Death." Neither sentimentality nor religious scruple interfered with the autopsy, an uncommon procedure at the time.

The family of James and Jane Hill Rundlet in Portsmouth, New Hampshire, grew in the usual pattern, with thirteen children born in the first twenty-six years of their marriage, the last when Jane Rundlet was forty-eight years old. When construction began on their fine new house in 1807, they had five children but were mourning their second son, Edward, who had died the previous January of "Quincey" at the age of eleven months. By the time their house was finished, two more sons had been born, but in 1810 eight-year-old Eliza died of spotted fever. Even within these large families each child was special, and the emotions surrounding death were powerful.

above

The mahogany stair rail at the Rundlet-May House in Portsmouth, New Hampshire, was no doubt an irresistible temptation for the Rundlets' twelve children.

left

The high post bed, matching crib, and cradle in the Rundlet-May House date from when babies were arriving every two years. The crib, moved to Jane Rundlet's side of the bed at night, allowed her to draw the baby into the warm bed for nursing.

When Richard and Mollie Tucker of Wiscasset, Maine, lost their fourth child, Matilda Wood, the grieving mother wrote that she was "the very loveliest of all, so sweet and bright, I never loved a child as well before. . . . " Matilda was buried in the Evergreen Cemetery; her tombstone has an image of a lamb and reads: "Another lamb now safely housed from life's tempestuous weather / Another angel joined the choir to sing God's praises forever."

Mollie, who had borne three children by the age of twenty, was badly affected by the stress of having many children plus an older husband whose "whole aim is to keep the wolf from the door and make my home happy" but who continually remodeled the house, tinkered with new inventions, and drank excessively. Apparently it was all more than Mollie could stand, for in 1879 she voluntarily entered a mental hospital and stayed there for a year, leaving her husband and five children, the youngest thirteen and the eldest twenty. The younger children were away attending school in the winter, but they returned to Wiscasset for active summers of swimming and sailing, theatricals, and parties.

When she came home, Mollie supplemented the family income by translating French books, writing plays from novels, and eventually taking in boarders, but she continued to express her discontent with her lot in life. "When I look about me at the girls of this town and think of mine, I feel that we belong to a different atmosphere—the restless wretched life I have led here from not being contented to adapt myself to these people bears its fruit for comfort in the forcing forth of my young family into a world which speedily formed them for better things than they could have found here. . . . It is far better to be ambitious and unhappy than to be commonplace and contented," she wrote in 1889 to her daughter Mame, an actress.

opposite

In 1883, when the Tucker children were teenagers, the family purchased a twenty-five-year-old pool table for $115. The snowy owl was caught in Castle Tucker's front yard in the 1870s by Richard Tucker III, whose collection of birds' eggs and other taxidermy is displayed in the billiard room.

The ten-pin alley in the barn at Roseland Cottage in Woodstock, Connecticut, was part of the original design, reflecting Henry Bowen's goal of creating a summer retreat with healthful activities to engage his children and family friends. At the Bowens' first Fourth of July celebration, in 1870, a delighted President Ulysses S. Grant threw a strike.

The ideal of family life in the mid-nineteenth century became more and more isolated from the world of industry and commerce, and rural retreats for summer living were highly prized by families who could afford them. At Roseland Cottage in Woodstock, Connecticut, far from the pressure of his trade as a dry goods merchant and journalist in Brooklyn, New York, Henry Bowen could participate in family activities, playing games with his eleven children and sixteen grandchildren, taking them for rides, and reading them stories. So sentimental was he about his grandchildren that he had their portraits painted as cherubs and mounted in ceiling medallions in his Brooklyn house; after his death family members framed them and brought them to Roseland.

Attitudes toward children had changed considerably by the end of the eighteenth century. Beginning to understand that childhood was a developmental stage rather than an expression of sinfulness, parents and teachers sought to study and guide children's emotional and intellectual growth. James and Jane Rundlet understood that play was children's work, and they provided books, musical instruments, and toys to foster learning and moral development.

A half century later children were perceived as innocent beings wholly dependent on adults for protection as well as nurture. Clothing styles exaggerated the differences between their world and that of adults. There were more toys, many of which reinforced gender-based expectations for adult roles and behavior. In wealthy families, children were often separated in nurseries and spent most of their time with hired nurses or governesses. This was the case with both the Lyman family in Waltham, Massachusetts, and the Codman family in Lincoln, Massachusetts.

right

Like other mothers, Ella Lyman felt the tug of emotions and powerful ties to the rooms of her Boston house, particularly the nursery.

When Ogden Codman Sr. fulfilled his dream of buying back his grandfather John Codman's house and land in Lincoln in 1862, he began at once to create an ideal rural retreat for his young family. Here the children—eventually five in all—had ponies and horses, played croquet, and enjoyed picnics, music, reading, and gardening. A beloved nurse, Reine, who joined the family during their sojourn in France, remained with them for forty years.

With the exception of Reine, turnover among Codman family servants was high. By the end of the nineteenth century, the role of servants had become much more formal. Increasingly drawn from the ranks of new immigrants, especially the Irish, live-in servants were no longer regarded as family members. The Codmans usually employed six servants at any one time: a cook, a chambermaid, a parlor maid, a nurse, and a kitchen maid who lived in and a manservant who came each day. But in 1872 alone they employed a total of four cooks, two parlor maids, and three chambermaids; sometimes servants walked out after only a few days. With a large house, large family, and regimented daily routine dependent on servants, the Codmans employed more than one hundred persons as servants while they lived at The Grange. Recruitment, training, and discipline of these people was a constant responsibility and, apparently, a constant source of disappointment for Sarah Codman.

Of the five Codman children, only Ogden Jr., the oldest, left The Grange to pursue a career and, eventually, to marry. After their mother died, the other four—Alice, Tom, Hugh, and Dorothy—pursued individual interests in music, photography, gardening, and filiopietism, never actively engaging with the world and apparently never throwing anything away.

right

Correspondence and
scrapbooks at the
Marrett House in
Standish, Maine,
document aspects
of Frances Marrett's
career as a teacher
of French and other
subjects at the Per-
kins School for the
Blind in Boston. The
photograph on the
left of the desk shows
her most famous
student, Helen Keller.

far right

The masculine third-
floor den of the
Rundlet-May House,
created by Dr. James
Rundlet May during
the 1890s, contains
his Civil War sword
as well as rowing
photographs and oars
that belonged to him
and his son Ralph,
both graduates of
Harvard University.

Like Dorothy Codman, who resided at The Grange until 1968, other unmarried New Englanders continued to live in the homes of their youth. Sarah Orne Jewett and her sister Mary moved into their grandfather's house in South Berwick, Maine, in 1888; Lucy Coffin lived alone at the Coffin House until 1893; and Mollie and Richard Tucker's daughter Jane lived on at Castle Tucker until 1964. Other families— the Bowens; the Mays, who inherited the Rundlet House in Portsmouth, New Hampshire; the Caseys, owners of the Casey Farm in Saunderstown, Rhode Island; and the Barretts, owners of Forest Hall in New Ipswich, New Hampshire—main- tained the old homesteads as summer retreats and places for family reunions. In 1889 the Marrett family gathered in Standish, Maine, to commemorate the centennial of the construction of their family home, and Frances Marrett returned to live there after she retired in the 1920s. In 1907 the Langdons reunited at the recently enlarged Governor John Langdon House in Portsmouth, New Hampshire, to celebrate the wedding of John Langdon's great-great-granddaughter Helen.

As family members dispersed in the nineteenth century, many kept in touch with the unmarried elderly cousins who lived on in the old family homesteads. Such was the case with Elizabeth Cheever Wheeler, who frequently returned to her great-great-grandfather Jonathan Sayward's house in York Harbor, Maine, to visit her cousins Elizabeth and Mary Barrell. When Mary Barrell died in 1889, she left the house to a nephew, but after his death in 1900 the future of the family homestead was uncertain. After considerable negotiation, Elizabeth Wheeler and her husband bought the old house and all its contents in 1901 to preserve it as "an ancestral place." The Wheelers worked closely with their architect to provide useful, comfortable spaces for their family, adding bathrooms, a large piazza, and new bedrooms with dormer windows in the attic. They installed new wallpaper and painted the wood-work a "colonial" white but left in place the furniture and historic relics that had been so treasured by their elderly cousins. With minimal change the house became the setting of summertime activity for the Wheelers and their four children for more than seventy years.

New Englanders' ideal of the extended family has remained inviolate since the colonial settlement of the region, when many generations lived together and raised children together. As prosperity allowed, families relied more on those outside the family to help with daily chores and child rearing, but family bonds remained strong. In the twentieth century, even as many family members moved farther away from the homestead, some returned to the family home, pulled to it by its history and the ties of a lifetime.

right

The Sayward-Wheeler House's riverside location in York Harbor, Maine, gave the Wheeler family ample opportunities for rowing, sailing, and fishing. The large piazza they added outside the parlor was the setting for many pleasant summer entertainments.

BACKSTAIRS LIFE

"The habit of calling from the top to the bottom of the house is sometimes permitted when only one servant is kept. It should never be allowed. . . . American voices have sufficient reputation for loudness and shrillness already, without increasing these unpleasant tendencies by screaming orders up or down a couple of flights of stairs."

Christine Terhune Herrick, *Housekeeping Made Easy*, 1888

A thick door at the bottom of the stairs (right) muffled sounds from the laundry room and the adjacent kitchen at Beauport in Gloucester, Massachusetts.

As America became more industrialized, the roles of the staff who kept New England households functioning began to change. The multigenerational homesteads of the eighteenth and early nineteenth centuries often included young girls who came to live with families to help with time-consuming and labor-intensive chores. Working side-by-side with the women of the house, these girls learned housekeeping skills to prepare them for running households of their own.

By the late nineteenth century, the industrial revolution opened up employment opportunities, and young women began working in mills, factories, and offices or for local merchants. Many found the regular wages, established work schedules, and freedom to live at home more desirable than the long hours, unpredictable demands, and loneliness that were part of live-in domestic service. Eleanor Hoyt Brainerd described the situation in 1910 in *The Ladies' Home Journal*:

The great reason why housework is repugnant to self-respecting Americans is not so much on account of the work itself, for other kinds of labor are hard and monotonous, but on account of the conditions under which it is performed. The single domestic lacks society; she is isolated from the family life and she can never call any time her own. Girls will work all day amid the steam of a laundry, the fumes of a factory, the bad air of a sewing-room, because there they have companionship, their hours are defined, and they are their own mistresses when the day's work is done.

At the same time that local girls were leaving domestic service, the number of immigrants arriving in New England's growing urban areas was increasing, filling the need for household workers. The tasks required to run a household also changed as people could more readily purchase many of their necessities. These shifts dramatically changed the relationship between families and their domestic help. No longer

below

At Castle Tucker in Wiscasset, Maine, the seventeen-year-old bride Mollie Tucker relied on hired help to keep the large home functioning.

were native-born girls, sometimes distant relatives or neighbors, sharing the burden of household chores. Strangers, often with unfamiliar backgrounds and customs, were joining households as domestic servants who worked for, not with, family members.

The shift from native-born to immigrant servants was slower outside larger New England cities such as Providence, Rhode Island; Hartford, Connecticut; and Boston. But even in smaller communities, the mistress-and-servant relationship underwent changes. In Wiscasset, Maine, Mollie Tucker often found managing her domestic servants a struggle. Mollie was only sixteen years old when she married Capt. Richard Tucker Jr. in 1857. After living for one year with Tucker's parents, the couple and their infant daughter moved into the imposing Lee Mansion, which became known as Castle Tucker. At only seventeen years old, Mollie found herself supervising servants who were often close to her own age. The Tuckers, a well-to-do but not excessively wealthy family at the time, typically employed only one or two domestics for housework and laundry. In correspondence with family members, Mollie regularly expressed her frustration with the women she hired. "I have great hopes of getting nicely provided for in the way of 'help' before March," she wrote to her traveling husband in December 1860. "I shall not certainly keep Sarah Jane. I am in constant anxiety about things which does not improve my rather defective amiabillity."

right

In need of additional income, Mollie Tucker opened Castle Tucker to summer boarders. Here a servant named Annie prepares the dining room for dinner about 1895.

The "servant problem" became a common challenge voiced by mistresses throughout the United States. Although servants were almost always blamed, more likely the responsibility should have been shared. In 1920 Christine Frederick counseled mistresses in *Household Engineering: Scientific Management in the Home:* "They may not outwardly admit it, but most women who are able to afford servants to assist them in the home, want those other women workers to stay *just servants* and to remain on a subordinate plane where they can be bossed and talked down to from her platform of the superior mistress. They want the 'servant' as well as the service."

Mollie Tucker continued to struggle with her mistress-servant relationships. "I sent Anna off today for good," she wrote to her mother in 1883, "& have another girl coming tomorrow. Anything will be a rest from her stupidity and carelessness. It takes so much patience to keep from scolding such girls & they are so provoking there was nothing else to do, but I trust to have bettered myself." The Tuckers' financial situation deteriorated over the years; by 1890 they began taking in boarders, a respectable way for women to earn income and a sensible way to take advantage of Maine's growing popularity with tourists. Although money was tight, the Tuckers still hired girls to assist with the increased work required to care for and feed their boarders. As Mollie wrote to her daughter in December 1889, "I keep Maggie which is an extravagance I admit all around but if I take boarders or lodgers next summer she is the best girl possible for me & to keep her for this purpose I must make this sacrifice not only of her wages, which I can ill afford, but the firewood & kerosene is a big item with the food also." Throughout the 1890s, a number of hired girls and at least one boy worked at Castle Tucker, but all stayed for only short periods of time.

The daily lives of the staff who kept New England households functioning differed depending on the needs of their employers, and their relationships varied as well. Mollie Tucker was demanding and required practical help in providing services to her boarders in coastal Maine, while at Beauport, in Gloucester, Massachusetts, Henry Davis Sleeper sought a different type of support for entertaining his guests.

From its inception in 1907, Beauport was intended to be a magical summer home where Sleeper could entertain his well-known and well-heeled friends, many of whom traveled from Boston and beyond to attend his lavish celebrations and costume parties. With five dining rooms and a breathtaking view of Gloucester Harbor, Beauport was active from spring until Thanksgiving. After struggling for several years to find dependable domestic servants for Beauport, in 1919 Sleeper hired Mary Wonson, who remained at Beauport until after his death in 1934.

right

Mary Wonson's room at Beauport was sparsely furnished but filled with light from a large window overlooking the house's front entrance.

left

**Mary Wonson (right)
oversees preparations
for one of the
McCann family's
dinners at Beauport
after they purchased
the property in 1935,
following Henry Davis
Sleeper's death.**

Mary Landergan Wonson was born in Allentown, Pennsylvania. Her father, John, was a coal miner who emigrated from Wales, and her mother, Flora, was from Antigonish, Nova Scotia. The family moved back to Nova Scotia when Mary was an infant. John soon abandoned the family, leaving Flora to support five small children. As was typical in working-class families, Mary was sent away to work. Shortly after completing the eighth grade, she went to live with her aunt in Somerville, Massachusetts, and began working as a day servant in the wealthy homes of Boston's Beacon Hill neighborhood, where she earned $3.50 per week.

In 1913 Mary married George Marble Wonson II of Gloucester. George was the caretaker at Red Roof, a summer home owned by the Harvard economist A. Piatt Andrew, two doors down from Beauport. One summer, Andrew recommended to his friend Sleeper that the Wonsons help at Beauport, an arrangement that lasted for more than four decades. The Wonsons eventually owned their own home in East Gloucester, but from early spring until early December they lived full time at Beauport, sharing two small rooms and a bathroom above the kitchen. Caring for the house was hard work, and they were on call all hours of the day and night: outside Mary's door was an annunciator, or a call box, that that Sleeper could use to signal the couple any time he required assistance.

far left

**Although the
McCanns replaced the
gas range when they
purchased the prop-
erty, little else was
changed in the Beau-
port kitchen.**

Beauport became the showcase for Sleeper's innovative interior designs, with articles on the property published as early as 1916. Mary's dedication to its care was exceptional. Each spring before Sleeper arrived from Boston, the Wonsons would open and prepare the home for the season. Before cleaning the 130-piece amber glass collection, Mary would meticulously sketch the arrangement. She would then bring the pieces to the kitchen for washing and return them to exactly where Sleeper had placed them. When Sleeper was not in residence, Mary would serve as tour guide, leading visitors through the museum-like interiors. Her commitment left a lasting impression on many who visited, including Henry Francis du Pont, who wrote on October 21, 1935, after Sleeper's death: "Another thing that struck me very much was the fact that that marvelous woman who used to look after the house for Henry Sleeper has kept it absolutely as though he is still living. I told her I thought it simply extraordinary the way she had retained the atmosphere of the house. At any moment I expected to see him walk into the room."

During Mary Wonson's brief time as a day servant in Boston before she came to Beauport, it is likely that many of the domestics with whom she worked were immigrants from Ireland or young, single, first-generation American women who received room and board as part of their compensation. Such was the case in Salem, Massachusetts, where the Phillips family was establishing its homestead at 34 Chestnut Street, once referred to by the English author P. D. James as "the most beautiful street in America." In June 1911 Anna Phillips purchased the elegant home for herself, her husband, Stephen Willard Phillips, and their young son, Stephen. The front four rooms of the Phillips House, dating from around 1800, were originally part of a house in nearby Danvers. Once moved to Salem in 1820–21, the house was expanded to include a third floor and a kitchen wing.

The Phillips family did not move into their new home right away. Instead they hired the architect William Rantoul to strip away the elaborate Victorian interiors that had been installed by previous owners and to remodel in the fashionable Colonial Revival style. The Phillipses moved in during the fall of 1912. A wealthy woman, Anna was descended from an old Salem family and was active in the community. Her husband was honorary curator of Pacific ethnology at Salem's Peabody Museum and later president of the Essex Institute. The couple frequently hosted luncheons and dinners in their home. By 1919 the family's busy lifestyle was supported by five servants, three of whom lived in the third-floor servants' quarters.

Sixteen-year-old Catherine Shaughnessy came to the United States in September 1897 from County Galway, in the west of Ireland. In 1910 she was hired by Anna Phillips, replacing a twenty-nine-year-old German woman as young Stephen's nursemaid. As was often the case with nursemaids, Catherine (who was referred to as "Cat" or "Catty" by the family) established a stronger bond with the young boy and his parents than did servants with other, less personal roles in the household. Catherine, who became an American citizen on June 20, 1927, lived with the Phillipses through 1965, long after young Stephen had grown and gone off to school and past the death of his father in 1955.

Once the Phillipses' son left for boarding school, Catherine served as a maid but remained close to him. Numerous letters survive from Stephen's years at Milton Academy, where she used to send him copies of his favorite comic strip, "Cap'n Stubbs." Anna wrote to her son on October 19, 1920: "Catherine has just brought the Captain Stubbs to put in this letter to you. I did not like to say I wouldn't, but I don't believe they would think it high toned literature at school. So you had better tear them up."

In 1918 Catherine was joined by another Irish-born servant, Delia Cawley, who was hired by the Phillipses as their waitress. Delia replaced a woman who left the Phillips family to marry. It was common for young women to work as live-in domestics only until they married and began caring for homes and families of their own. Born in Tubercurry, in northwestern Ireland, Delia came to the United States in 1891. Her first job was as a live-in maid for Daniel Low of Salem. When the Lows moved, Delia came to work for the Phillips family, increasing her wages from $3 to $5 per week. On February 13, Anna wrote in her calendar, "New waitress, Delia Cawley."

Delia was in charge of the china closet. She would set the table, serve meals, wash the dishes, and wash and iron linens. Although she never married, Delia did have family responsibilities outside the Phillips home. In 1916 her sister Mary died, leaving five children and her husband, Thomas Lyons, who never remarried. Every evening after finishing her chores for the Phillipses, she would walk to her brother-in-law's home to care for the children, bringing groceries and preparing food for the following day. At fifty-seven years old, Delia became an American citizen on the same day as Catherine Shaughnessy. Delia worked for the Phillips family for thirty-one years.

The longevity of the Phillipses' staff was most unusual for the time, when domestic servants frequently changed households for higher wages or better living conditions. Richard A. Wells wrote in 1894, in *Manners Culture and Dress of the Best of American Society:*

In this country, servants are proverbially more troublesome than in Europe, where service is often transmitted through generations in one family. Here, the housekeeper is obliged to change often, taking frequently the most ignorant of the lower classes of foreigners to train into good and useful servants, only to have them become dissatisfied as soon as they become acquainted with others, who instil the republican doctrine of perfect equality into their minds, ruining them for good servants.

above

The back staircase at the Phillips House gave access from the kitchen to the third-floor servants' rooms.

left

The Phillipses added this china closet during their 1911–12 renovations. It served as a buffer between the noisy kitchen and the dining room.

The Phillipses' cook, Bridget Durgin, would begin her day early by descending the servants' stairs, starting a fire in the stove, and preparing breakfast for the family.

Anna Phillips had the most difficulty finding and keeping dependable cooks, perhaps because of the family's elaborate menus and frequent entertaining. On June 20, 1919, she noted in her calendar that the cook, Kitty, had been "Paid in full," clearly ending her employment with the family. Kitty was replaced by Bridget Durgin (or Durkin), who came to the United States from Ireland in the 1880s. Bridget was with the Phillips family for five years, until February 13, 1925, when she died suddenly while walking on Chestnut Street. Shortly thereafter, Anna wrote to her son: "I haven't got a cook yet but hope to by tomorrow. I am getting tired of going out to all my meals and Catherine is getting tired of doing the little cooking she has to do and I miss her upstairs."

Catherine, Delia, and Bridget each had her own heated room in the Phillips household and shared a bathroom on the third floor. As was typical of domestic servants of the day, the women who worked for the Phillips family lived in, and the men on their staff kept their own homes and came daily to work. Cornelius "Con" Flynn began working for the family as a coachman before its move to Chestnut Street. Con, whose parents emigrated from Ireland, was born in a waterfront neighborhood of Salem. He stayed on as the Phillipses' caretaker and groundskeeper after the introduction of the automobile made the role of coachman obsolete. The family's first chauffeur, Patrick O'Hara, was also born and raised in Salem. The Phillipses began renting automobiles around 1910, and Patrick stayed employed with the family into the 1920s, shifting from driving rented vehicles to driving and caring for Stephen Willard Phillips's Pierce-Arrows—a true symbol of how the industrial revolution changed the lives of New Englanders forever.

right

Patrick O'Hara, the Phillipses' chauffeur, took Anna Phillips (standing), the nursemaid, Catherine Shaughnessy, and young Stephen Phillips on an excursion about 1913.

COMFORT AND CONVENIENCE

"Every time I come back to Berwick I am so eager to know

what I can do for it—but the little town is so unconscious of

possible betterments, and goes on . . . so comfortably, . . .

that it is like a sleeping beauty in its wood."

Sarah Orne Jewett, undated letter to Annie Fields

In 1903 a new bathroom for Sarah Codman's bedroom was installed in the Codman House in Lincoln, Massachusetts, replacing one forty years old.

Residents of Sarah Orne Jewett's hometown of South Berwick, Maine, reflected the conservatism and frugality of many nineteenth-century New Englanders. Although some families accepted new household technologies as soon as they could afford them, others doggedly kept to their old ways despite the potential for increased comfort and convenience. By the end of the century, rustic life was eagerly adopted by some city dwellers during their summers in the country, but as soon as the season turned cold they hurried back to the central heat, running water, bathroom fixtures, and gaslight or electricity of their city homes. At the Hamilton House in South Berwick, Maine, the Marrett House in Standish, Maine, and the Sayward-Wheeler House in York Harbor, Maine, as at many others, old-fashioned technology was preserved for new generations as evidence of family unity, triumph over adversity, and a prudent way of life.

far left

The kitchen sink at Castle Tucker in Wiscasset, Maine, was set in a cabinet built by a local shipbuilder, the water pumped to it from a cellar cistern. The adjacent Hoosier kitchen cabinet, advertised as step-saving, was bought for $25 in 1920.

left

Lamps in attic storage at the Hamilton House in South Berwick, Maine, include kerosene and whale oil lamps, some adapted with electrical fittings for use in this Colonial Revival home. The attic's main lighting is an electric wall sconce with a pull chain from about 1925.

Most families relied on fireplaces well into the early 1800s as a source of heat and a place to cook, even though they allowed large quantities of heat to escape directly up the chimney. Having no alternatives, each year families cut, split, and consumed vast quantities of wood. In July 1790 Jonathan Sayward of York Harbor noted that his family had burned forty-four cords of wood during the previous twelve months, a fairly typical amount for cooking and heating in a good-sized house. So grateful was the Reverend Daniel Marrett to receive his winter's wood supply from members of his Standish congregation in the 1790s that in return he rewarded them with alcoholic beverages and food: "two pails of grog, a pail of flip, and a supper of baked pudding and boiled victuals."

In all these houses, the large kitchen fireplace with its broad hearth was the center of intense activity. In 1839, when Caleb Huse was eight years old, he had gone to live in the Coffin House in Newbury, Massachusetts. Two years earlier his father had remarried into the Coffin family. Reminiscing about the house sixty-two years later, Huse wrote to his niece Marjorie Huse:

I remember distinctly the great fireplace in the kitchen, which was the room back of the 'sitting room,' and opening into it. On the opposite side was the great fireplace, and at the right as you entered was the Dresser, with its shelves well filled with very bright pewter platters[,] plates and 'porringers'—an article of housekeeping quite gone out, I believe, with the skillet and the crane from which big 'pot hooks' and 'Trammels' hung the 'pots' and kettles—which differed from each other.

The kitchen that Huse so fondly recalled, already more than a century and a half old when he first saw it, was dominated by the cavernous fireplace filled with heavy black iron pots. A large, domed "beehive" oven at the side of the fireplace opening was used for weekly baking; occasionally quick breads and single pies might be baked in a covered iron kettle buried in coals on the hearth. Here in the kitchen food was cooked or processed to be preserved through the winter; water was heated for making tea, laundering, dishwashing, and bathing; tallow was melted for candle dipping; and family members, hired help, traveling strangers, and friendly neighbors gathered to enjoy the warmth of the fire and one another's company. So compelling are the images of the kitchen fireplace in defining the New England domestic experience that enlarged and overfurnished kitchen fireplaces—sometimes nonfunctional—are still being constructed in houses across America.

right

Built shortly after 1700, the "new" kitchen at the Coffin House in Newbury, Massachusetts, features a large cooking fireplace. Opposite is a built-in dresser, or cupboard, used to store and display the family's pewter dinnerware, which through reflection increased the amount of light in the room.

left

In the huge fireplace of Beauport's Pine Kitchen in Gloucester, Massachusetts, Henry Sleeper installed a superfluity of cooking equipment. This look helped set the style for thousands of museum exhibitions—referred to by Abbott Lowell Cummings as "culinary obstacle courses"—many so cluttered that no meal could be successfully prepared there.

opposite

Among many other items, Henry Sleeper collected New England redware pottery. The color harmonies of the redware, pewter, and green-handled cutlery are typical of Sleeper's arrangements at Beauport.

The New England kitchen's productivity and functionality appealed to early-twentieth-century proponents of the Colonial Revival style such as Henry Davis Sleeper. In 1917 at his summer home, Beauport, in Gloucester, Massachusetts, he designed and had built what is perhaps the most artful and widely imitated early presentation of this ideal—a room known as the Pembroke Room, or the Pine Kitchen. Larger than any eighteenth-century kitchen, this room boasts a central sitting area and several dining spaces, but its focal point is a huge fireplace with an overabundance of attractive cooking equipment. Sleeper's interpretation of the colonial kitchen had much to do with establishing the misleading image of the typical colonial hearth still popular today. The Pine Kitchen was frequently illustrated in home magazines, and Sleeper replicated it for many of his interior design clients, including Henry Francis du Pont, whose own Pine Kitchen at the Winterthur Museum in Delaware remained intact until 1959.

Despite their symbolic value, many colonial hearths were replaced in the nineteenth century by more efficient technologies that did not waste fuel or labor. Improved fireplaces and cooking devices grew out of new scientific understanding of the nature of heat and combustion. The most influential inventor of such equipment was Benjamin Thompson, later Count Rumford, who in the 1790s published a series of illustrated essays on the subject. Rumford promoted the use of both built-in masonry ranges with individual boilers and a sheet-iron roasting device in which temperature and humidity could be controlled and kept constant.

At Castle Tucker in
Wiscasset, Maine,
an Empire Crawford
woodstove was
installed in 1905 in
the spot where
cooking had always
been done—directly
in front of the kitchen
fireplace. The iron
door at the right gave
access to the brick
oven, which could
still be used.

right

The Rumford cooking
apparatus at the
Rundlet-May House in
Portsmouth, New
Hampshire, is one of
the most complete in
existence. The round
iron door opens into
the roaster, in which
steam and heat could
be regulated by
means of knobs and
handles; steam
escaped into the vent
above. The original
fire pits and ash pits
are behind the iron
doors under the adja-
cent modern counter.

One of the most complete early kitchens in New England incorporating Rumford's ideas is found at the Rundlet-May House in Portsmouth, New Hampshire. The roaster, made by John Badger, and the masonry stove with three boilers, installed by Henry Cates, cost more than $120 in 1808, when a simple iron cookstove might be priced as low as $20. Cooking with such equipment required an entirely different set of skills from working at an open hearth. Apparently Jane Rundlet, her daughters, and her hired help were able to manage this, for bills indicate that repair work was done as late as 1858. By that time much simpler cookstoves were readily available.

Hundreds of patents for cookstoves document minor changes in technology through the 1800s as people sought to improve fuel efficiency, save time and labor, and make stoves ornaments to the kitchen. By the end of the century, the freestanding cast-iron cookstove, designed to use wood or coal, had replaced the open hearth in most New England kitchens. Often the opening of the old cooking fireplace was sealed and the new cookstove positioned directly in front of it on the wide hearth. At Castle Tucker, in Wiscasset, Maine, Mollie Tucker's 1858 Stewart cookstove was superseded in 1905 by the Empire Crawford stove that remains in place today. This stove was promoted by its manufacturer as responding to housekeepers' desires for simpler stoves "at once plain and shapely," with a minimum of nickel-plated trim to polish.

The buttery at the
Coffin House was
a northern room—
the first floor's cool-
est room—suitable
for dairying in the
spring, summer, and
early fall and for food
storage at any time.

As soon as gas and then electricity became available, many families removed their large iron cookstoves and replaced them with stoves using these labor-saving fuels. In contrast, the Tuckers kept theirs in place when in 1926 they bought a Campbell automatic rapid electric fireless cooker range, whose manufacturer claimed that it would save time, money, work, and worry. This small stove has just two full-sized hot plates on the top but features two important innovations: a fireless cooker and an oven in which heat could be automatically controlled by a thermostat. Hailed as "the cheapest and most satisfactory method of cooking all foods that can be cooked by boiling, steaming and stewing," the fireless cooker used only "enough electricity to start the food boiling"; it then automatically shut itself off while the food "continued to cook without expense or attention of any kind," retaining heat in the insulated cooking chamber. The Campbell stove plugged into a standard wall outlet and used home lighting circuits.

Without electric refrigeration, people depended on naturally cool cellars, wells, and northern rooms to preserve food and beverages. Butteries, or dairy rooms, were functional small rooms, located on the cool northern side of the house and lined with many shelves to hold the broad redware milk pans in which cream would be set to rise. Caleb Huse recalled that the Coffin House buttery was "always as clean and sweet as possible," but in summer, when cheese making was under way, the buttery would be filled with strong odors that attracted insects and rodents. In winter, food and water stored here would freeze solid.

For food preservation, cool summer drinks, and ice cream, ice was required. From about 1860 on, some families, such as the Bowens in Woodstock, Connecticut, had icehouses in which to store a supply of natural ice cut from local ponds. Others, among them the Tuckers in Wiscasset, Maine, relied on regular delivery of blocks of ice that had been commercially harvested.

above

The electric Campbell
range purchased for
Castle Tucker in 1926
allowed the family to
cook with carefully
and easily regulated
heat. The drawerlike
lower section, the
"fireless cooker,"
used no electricity
during cooking but
relied on heat stored
in the range's insu-
lated compartment.

At Castle Tucker two
iceboxes were kept
against a cold north
wall in an unheated
shed. The taller of
these insulated
chests, a type known
as the Eddy refriger-
ator, was made in
1905 in Boston.

Just as technical innovations transformed cooking methods, household heating also changed. Huge central chimneys, like the one at the Coffin House, retained some heat and radiated it throughout the house, but their fireplaces had damperless openings that sent a large proportion of their heat directly outdoors. Rooms were heated unevenly and thus were often uncomfortably warm next to the fire while below freezing against the windows. Doors to hallways, bedchambers, pantries, closets, and attics were kept closed in winter; temperatures in these rooms could remain below freezing for weeks or months at a time. Count Rumford's suggestions for smaller, shallower fireboxes that would radiate more heat into the rooms and for smoke shelves inside the chimney that would prevent downdrafts were soon widely understood by New England masons. Most nineteenth-century chimneys, like those at the Rundlet-May House, reflect an understanding of this advice in one form or another.

In mid-December 1858, shortly after Richard and Mollie Tucker had moved into Castle Tucker, they entertained Richard's father, who wrote about the visit: "[W]e were over there to tea last eve, all pleasant except the cold … need many airtights [stoves]." Three weeks later another family member described the situation: "Richard is very successful in warming his house, has a large coal stove in the hall, one in dining room, and a stove in the north parlor, keeping the air at nearly an even temperature throughout. He has put in double windows all through." Even these stoves and the storm windows were not enough to counteract the cold of a Maine winter, however, and by the end of the month Tucker had designed and installed a furnace in the cellar. It must have helped, for Mollie wrote in March 1859: "I do not think I could live in this house without a fire in that cellar in winter, it is very damp."

The furnaces installed in the Rundlet-May House and Castle Tucker in the mid-nineteenth century conveyed heated air to the first floor only. At Roseland Cottage in Woodstock, Connecticut, a similar coal-fired "spider" furnace, so called because of its many leglike ducts, was installed in the 1920s, when members of the family first began to live there year-round. In all three of these houses, heat rose to the second floor only by way of the staircases. At Castle Tucker members of each generation expanded and contracted their living space in response to the changing seasons. During the winter months, they closed off the main block of the house and lived in the smaller, more easily heated rooms of the low-ceilinged ell, comprising the dining room, kitchen, and two rooms above, as well as the small first-floor sitting room, using it as a downstairs bedroom.

opposite

In the stair hall at Castle Tucker, the hole made by the installation of a stove pipe in the cold winter of 1858–59, when Richard and Mollie Tucker first lived there, is now closed with a round tin cover.

above

The huge ducts of the 1920s "spider" furnace at Roseland Cottage in Woodstock, Connecticut, have been severed but once carried hot air to the first-floor rooms.

opposite top

Once the new ell at
the Marrett House in
Standish, Maine, was
constructed in 1840,
family members did
not have to go out-
side to use the privy.
The multiple seats
were convenient—
especially the low
one for children—
but what etiquette or
hierarchy governed
their use is unknown.

right

The muddy kitchen
dooryard at the Casey
Farm in Saunders-
town, Rhode Island,
photographed by
Harry Weir Casey in
the late 1870s, shows
the dangerous
proximity of waste
disposal, animal
excrement, and the
fresh water supply.
Undoubtedly dish-
pans, washbasins,
and washtubs were
emptied close to the
well and rain barrel.

Equally as critical to daily life as cooking and heating is the availability of clean
water. Most seventeenth- and eighteenth-century New England households relied on
dug wells and rain barrels for their water supplies. Wastewater was discarded in the
dooryard or simply thrown out the window, and privies were built in convenient albeit
sometimes indiscreet locations. At the Spencer-Peirce-Little Farm, archaeologists
have excavated a privy located only fifty feet from the front door. At the nearby Coffin
House, a freestanding privy was also built close to the main house; apparently the
downhill drainage made the site ideal. As the quest for gentility increased, a greater
sense of order was imposed, and privies were often built at the end of an attached ell,
as at the Rundlet-May House and Roseland Cottage and at the Marrett House when
it was renovated in 1840. Like many other families, the Marretts had a three-hole
privy with one lower seat to accommodate the children.

opposite bottom

The Coffin House's
freestanding privy
(left) had good
drainage. Still, to get
to it, residents had to
cross the open door-
yard, regardless of
the weather. The
original single-seat
privy at the Rundlet-
May House (right),
built at the beginning
of the nineteenth
century, reflects some
striving for privacy.

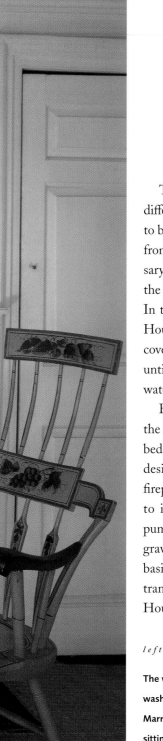

The necessity of hand carrying water from a well certainly was one reason for a different standard of personal cleanliness. Until the early 1800s, little attention was paid to bathing the entire body. Most New Englanders used only a small amount of water from a washbasin or kitchen skillet to clean their hands, face, neck, or feet as necessary. At the end of the previous century a new piece of furniture had been designed: the washstand, which held a basin of water and provided a shelf for towels and soap. In the sitting-room chamber (the bedroom above the sitting room) of the Marrett House, the washstand is conveniently placed by the fireplace and is equipped with a covered slop bucket to hold the contents of the chamber pot or the used bathwater until carried downstairs; the pot's contents were poured into the privy, while the bathwater was thrown into the garden.

Bathing had become a more commonly accepted practice by the mid-nineteenth century. Many people used portable tubs in bedchambers, but some houses had small rooms specifically designated as bathing rooms. Remarkably few of these had fireplaces. Roseland Cottage had such a room, but no pipes led to it. Rainwater was collected in a basement cistern and pumped to another cistern in the attic, from which it flowed by gravity to the kitchen, where it was heated and then carried in basins, buckets, or jugs to the bathing room, much as it was transported to the bedchambers of Castle Tucker, the Marrett House, and many other houses of the period.

left

The washstand and washbasin in the Marrett House's sitting-room chamber were placed in a sunny spot near the fireplace. Family members could be warmed by the fire while taking a sponge bath.

below

J. C. Wells's 1846 architectural plan for Roseland Cottage shows the convenient arrangement of the bathing room, washroom, kitchen, wood house, and privies, reflecting the mid-nineteenth-century's attention to the full complement of domestic service spaces.

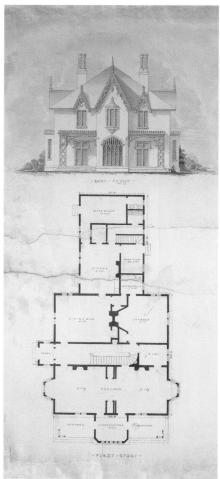

left

Next to cleanliness ranked good grooming. Silver accoutrements line the dresser top in a chamber at the Merwin House in Stockbridge, Massachusetts.

opposite

At the Barrett House in New Ipswich, New Hampshire, a new bathing room was constructed shortly before 1916 to receive this elaborate shower bath with multiple controls that would have sent water all around the bather.

Bathrooms with water closets and running water had been installed in some New England houses, including Roseland Cottage and the Codman House in Lincoln, Massachusetts, by the end of the nineteenth century. In 1903 Sarah Codman spent more than $3,600 to update a bathroom that had been installed forty years earlier. At about the same time, Elizabeth and George Barrett began renovating their house, Forest Hall, in New Ipswich, New Hampshire, but the elaborate bathroom fixtures they ordered never shed a drop of water. Elizabeth died in 1911 and George in 1916, leaving the work unfinished. The elaborate shower they had ordered was never hooked up to the new plumbing and has never been used.

left

Richard and Mollie Tucker's family apothecary case, or medicine kit, which dates from the 1850s, still holds seventy glass vials with cork lids. It also retains the original paper label listing seventy-six drugs, including five "Diptheria Medicines" and four "Tinctures."

The set kettle and an auxiliary fireplace in the summer kitchen at the Rundlet-May House were useful for laundry as well as for all sorts of food processing chores. A summer kitchen kept the heat generated by these activities out of the main house during hot weather.

right

Except in the most carefully designed landscapes, laundry lines were a visible weekly feature outside every New England home. This watercolor shows a typical scene at the Jackson House in Portsmouth, New Hampshire, between 1880 and 1910.

A much larger supply of clean water has always been needed for laundry than for personal hygiene. Until hot and cold running water was available indoors, until electricity could be relied on to agitate and wring out the laundry, and until the used water could be quickly drained away from the work area, the weekly wash day was dreaded, especially in the cold winter months. Laundry was the task most frequently delegated to the help, but it was always closely supervised. Typically done outside in all but the coldest weather, laundry involved heating at least thirty gallons of water; standing in mud while working with lye soaps and bleach; boiling clothes and bedding; rubbing and scrubbing badly soiled work clothes, aprons, diapers, and sickbed linens; paying special attention to small and delicate items such as collars and cuffs; lifting, wringing, and spreading out to dry the heavy wet items; bringing things in before they were soiled by birds or blown away in an unexpected gale; putting away the heavy tubs, wash bench, and scrubbing boards; and being ready to mend and iron the next day. By 1825 some houses had large, built-in kettles that were particularly useful for doing laundry. The rear kitchen of the Rundlet-May House, which is adjacent to the main kitchen and yet located near the well, has such a kettle. With thirteen children born in this family, twelve of them surviving infancy, enormous quantities of laundry must have been done in this room.

At the Codman House a new service ell was added in 1885 containing a kitchen with a built-in range and a separate laundry room with three set tubs (washtubs with fixed bases and legs), a wringer, a washboard, and two pails. Room was also made for two ironing tables with smooth blanket-covered surfaces and a starch kettle. The drying room next door contained two clothes racks, a small coal stove, eight irons, and an iron stand. Radiant heat from the adjacent kitchen chimney was used to speed the drying process, and the stove for cooking starch and heating irons was vented through a pipe inserted into the chimney. At Roseland Cottage in 1870 a similar laundry room with three set tubs replaced an earlier room in the cellar. Most laundry rooms had windows, and the work was usually done during daylight hours.

For their sources of light throughout the colonial period, New Englanders relied primarily on sunshine, moonlight, firelight, and candles. Because artificial light was considered an indulgence, candles were rarely lighted during daylight hours, and many households relied on only a single candle or firelight alone to extend the day. After the 1789 invention of the Argand burner for whale-oil lamps, the amount of light generated by a single source increased from one to as many as six candlepower, and the use of shades was considered necessary. Argand mantel lamps were usually luxuries, made in fashionable designs of expensive materials. Whether they used oil lamps or candles, few people kept lights burning in hallways or other fixed locations. Lights were usually moved to wherever they would be needed. In the Rundlet-May House and the few others where fixed lighting devices were installed, the flames were carefully protected by glass shades.

For many people the first real improvement in household lighting followed the development of kerosene in the 1850s. Refined from petroleum, kerosene burned more brightly than whale oil and was soon both widely available and inexpensive. Kerosene lamps had to be refilled, their wicks trimmed, and their chimneys washed frequently, but they soon replaced candles as the standard source of light in most households in rural and small-town New England.

Despite the innovations designed to increase comfort, convenience, and cleanliness, few really saved time or reduced labor until supported by reliable plumbing and electrical systems. Electricity was first installed at Castle Tucker in 1915, bringing lights only to a few prime spots: the barn, hall, dining room, kitchen, and front door. The Bowen family relied on kerosene lamps until 1920, when Roseland Cottage was fully electrified. Electric appliances soon followed, with refrigerators, washing machines, stoves, and irons appearing in even the oldest kitchens.

In the early 1940s Ise Gropius found the new technology in her modern home helpful when jobs in war-related industries lured away her household staff. Reflecting on that time, she wrote in her history of the Gropius House (1977):

The standard kitchen and pantry equipment—white glazed metal cabinets, kitchen range and refrigerator, did not ever have to be replaced. In 1938 the General Electric Co. offered us as a present the installation of a dishwasher in the pantry and a garbage disposal in the kitchen because they had difficulty selling these items at that time to the public and expected to get

free advertising if they were seen in a house that would attract many visitors. Everyone warned us not to have them installed because a maid would always be too fearful to use the machines. They were right in that assumption but when the maids walked into the highly paid munitions factory jobs in 1941, I was one of the few housewives well equipped to cope with the new situation.

Despite New Englanders' nostalgia for the old ways, few relied for long on antiquated technology in the kitchen and the laundry room. Soft candlelight created a colonial ambiance, but bright bedside reading lamps, central heating, and electric stoves, refrigerators, and washing machines followed rural electrification into New England homes as the twentieth century progressed. As a result, houses were brighter and people were cleaner and more comfortable. New Englanders appreciated the clever principles on which the new appliances operated, their energy efficiency, and their thrifty operation. They had been applying such principles to domestic technology for generations—but never with such results.

above

When the Gropius House was completed in 1938, its kitchen— tiny but augmented by an unusually large window—featured many innovative labor-saving devices. The stark white and stainless steel are relieved by colorful pot holders of Marimekko fabric.

AT THE TABLE

"And now they for their morning meal,

Pull out the table, lay the cloth,

And fondly to each other deal,

Some tempting dish, perhaps some broth.

This done they put the things away,

Each in its own accustomed place."

Anonymous Maine poet, early 1880s

left

Jonathan Sayward's valuable and useful silver cann, porringer, and tankard were engraved with his initials so that they could be readily identified if stolen from his home in York Harbor, Maine.

Food was a central part of daily life in New England, a fact captured in the doggerel verse describing Elizabeth and Mary Barrell's breakfast habits in their great-grandfather Jonathan Sayward's house in York Harbor, Maine, in the early 1880s. Even for these impoverished elderly sisters, mealtime was more than an activity to fuel the body; it also perpetuated the lifelong routines of setting up and taking down a table, spreading a clean tablecloth, and finding pleasure in each other's enjoyment of simple foods. Planning, preparing, and serving wholesome and delicious meals have always required much time and energy, but people have invariably found ways to enhance the experience of eating with cherished rituals, ornamental tablewares, and social interaction.

The ways of serving food and the type of utensils used varied with economic and social status. In the seventeenth and eighteenth centuries, rural families expected most meals to be served from a single large pewter platter, similar to those at the Coffin House, and to eat them with spoons, knife blades, or their fingers; forks were a rarity. Dinner was usually the main meal of the day, served sometime in the early afternoon, while a lighter meal, often called tea or supper, was served in the early evening.

As mistress of the old stone house now known as the Spencer-Peirce-Little House in Newbury, Massachusetts, a recently impoverished Mrs. Nathaniel Tracy attempted to keep up appearances. When visited by Alice Tucker "just at dusk" on the evening of October 20, 1789, she was "dress'd genteelly, sitting at her tea table with her children about her." When Miss Tucker visited again a little more than a year later, on December 13, 1790, she noted in her diary:

As soon as we got to their yard a neat looking maid came out to open the gate for us, and conducted us into the house and into the dining chamber, which is spacious and has a genteel and airy appearance considering its antiquity. Mrs. Tracy received us with that politeness which is so natural to a well bred woman. Our repast was slender; two cups of tea and one small piece of biscuit.

opposite

Among the objects in the Sayward-Wheeler House's "beaufat" are six Chinese export porcelain plates in the Imari style. Jonathan Sayward brought them back in 1745 as booty from the American expedition against the French fortress of Louisburg in Canada.

pages 172–73

In 1867 Richard Tucker traveled to Philadelphia and bought a 152-piece gold-banded Haviland dinner set, including a custard stand with twelve matching covered cups. Today Mollie Tucker's prized possession is displayed with other Tucker family glass and china at Castle Tucker, their home in Wiscasset, Maine.

Rarely was a specific room designated as a dining room throughout much of the eighteenth century. It was not uncommon, in fact, for tea to be served or meals to be taken in any of several rooms, even on occasion in bedchambers. Estate inventories, by listing quantities and locations of articles associated with food preparation and service, document some of the ways in which these were used. When Josiah Quincy of Quincy, Massachusetts, died in 1784, his estate inventory revealed that the pewter plates were kept in the kitchen while the more fragile—and valuable—glass and china were kept in the "East Lower Room," apparently where they were used and possibly where they were washed and dried afterward. The tablecloths and napkins were kept in a chest in an unfinished second-floor room. The Quincy family owned silver forks, fruit knives, wine and sweetmeat glasses, soup plates, five teapots, and assorted pieces of the cream-colored tableware called Queensware. The most elaborate item was a glass pyramid, a group of three graduated glass stands designed to be placed one on another; glasses of fruit or wine jellies and sweetmeats were displayed on such stands throughout a meal before being eaten as dessert. The tea table was kept in yet another room, suggesting that the first room was used for dinner and the other for tea. In these arrangements the Quincy family adhered to the cultural norms for people of their wealth and station.

In 1797 Mrs. Tracy sold her old stone house in Newbury to Capt. Offin Boardman and his second wife, Sarah Tappan. Offin's diary describes a variety of entertainments such as one held on the evening of October 22, 1799, when "a company" of thirty people came to finish husking corn and was served roast mutton and puddings before going home at half past one in the morning. The Boardmans sometimes gave dinner parties for fifteen or twenty people on winter afternoons when the sleighing was good. In 1803 they began to hold large tea parties for thirteen to thirty people, and on October 14, 1808, they entertained eighty at supper. Boardman's diary gives no clue about how many servants they employed or whether he and his wife adhered to the custom of separating men and women into different rooms and having their servants pass the teacups and plates of cake around circles of seated guests, but this was a common New England practice at the time.

left

At the Coffin House in Newbury, Massachusetts, as at the homes of many of their contemporaries, the Coffin family did not set aside a room exclusively for dining. The table in the north parlor, probably kept folded against the wall when not in use, could be moved to the center of the room for any meal.

left

Some of the Rundlets'
glass is arranged on
their sideboard in the
"sublime crescents"
recommended by
Robert Roberts. He
advised: "In setting
out your sideboard,
you must study neat-
ness, convenience,
and taste…. I have
often seen at parties
where I have been
attending, side boards
and side tables set out
in such a manner that
they looked quite in
a state of confusion;
whereas, if they were
set out in a proper
order, they would
make a magnificent
appearance."

It became more common in the early 1800s for a specific room to be designated as a dining room and furnished with a sideboard and a large number of chairs. New kinds of dining tables could be adjusted to serve various numbers of diners, and people began to purchase large dinner services in matching patterns. Tea and coffee wares were made of finer and more fragile materials, often porcelain, and tea continued to be served in parlors and bedchambers rather than in dining rooms. At the home of James and Jane Rundlet in Portsmouth, New Hampshire, the "Blue Liverpool" dinner service consisted of dinner, soup, and dessert plates, as well as a soup tureen and ladle and a salad bowl. A porcelain tea and coffee service had teacups, straight-sided coffee cups, and deep saucers that could be used with either type of cup. These ceramic wares were augmented by an extensive assortment of glassware and silverware, including a silver teapot, sugar bowl, and cream pot made in London by Peter and William Bateman.

With the introduction of dining rooms and more specialized forms of furniture and crockery, the rituals of entertaining became more formal. In 1827 Robert Roberts, a black butler who had worked for several prominent Massachusetts families, including Christopher and Rebecca Gore, published *The House Servant's Directory*, a manual of advice for those "entering into gentleman's service." Covering everything from house-cleaning to making lemonade, with special attention given to master-servant rela-tionships and the patterns of service at tea and dinner parties, Roberts's book quickly set standards for cleanliness, food service, and servant behavior. Roberts perfectly understood the importance of predictable service and the prestige derived from a dis-play of expensive tablewares. The principles he articulated seem to have been widely accepted by prosperous New England families such as the Rundlets and were emulated even by people who relied on a small number of servants lacking formal training.

far left

The southwest room
of the Rundlet-May
House in Portsmouth,
New Hampshire, with
its original "Green
Worm" wallpaper and
Rundlet furniture,
glass, and dinner-
ware, was originally
used as a dining
room. The table is set
for the dessert course
of a dinner party.

Large, formal dinner parties were common at the Boston home of Congressman Harrison Gray Otis and his wife, Sally, in the late eighteenth century. John Quincy Adams once wrote that in all his experience in America and Europe he had never met a man as skilled in the art of entertaining his friends as Harry Otis. Famous as a connoisseur of fine food and wines, Otis was renowned for his dinner parties. In an 1815 letter to Sally, then in Philadelphia, he described a dinner party he was giving on May 30 for twenty fellow Federalists in honor of Theodore Lyman of Waltham, Massachusetts. Otis himself would sit at the head of the table, and in Sally's absence Lyman, as the guest of honor, would be seated opposite him. The first course—lamb, salmon, pie, ham, soup, and chickens arranged symmetrically around a platter of mutton—would be followed by a course of salads with cheese and bread and butter; wines would be served throughout the meal. After these courses the tablecloth would be removed, dessert and fruit plates set at each place, and the desserts served with additional wines.

**The table in the
Harrison Gray Otis
House in Boston
is set according to
Roberts's rules. The
crumb cloth beneath
the table remained in
place throughout
dinner and dessert to
protect the wall-to-
wall carpet from
spilled wine and food.**

Tea for the women would be brought to the withdrawing room after they had left the dining room. Such elaborate service implied familiarity with socially correct table manners. At this dinner, Otis invited his fourteen- and fifteen-year-old sons, James and William, to sit nearby on opposite sides of a sideboard, possibly to observe and learn these niceties.

Roberts's guidebook for house servants was only one of a host of cookbooks and instructional volumes that helped Americans become familiar with more sophisticated foods, good manners, and the expectations of polite society. American authors responded quickly to the new demand for advice books. Among the most popular were Lydia Maria Child's *American Frugal Housewife* (1832) and Catherine Beecher's *Treatise on Domestic Economy* (1841), both tailored for middle-class women. Jane Rundlet owned the *Cook's Oracle and Housekeeper Manual: Receipts for Cooking and Directions for Carving*, published in 1830, after she had been married and running a household for thirty-five years; it is unclear whether the book was acquired as a source of new ideas or for the instruction of her four daughters, who were then in their twenties. Sarah Codman cherished her mother's copy of *Domestic Duties or Instructions for Young Married Ladies* (1828), which included guidelines for household management and interior decoration in addition to recipes and remedies. These books and others like them defined for many the nineteenth-century domestic ideal of a home run by a well-organized woman for her husband and children, a home in which most of the heavy work was done by servants.

left

**Ladies being enter-
tained by Harry and
Sally Otis would retire
after dinner to the
withdrawing room
on the second floor.
Here they would
enjoy a cup of tea
while the gentlemen
remained in the
dining room below for
brandy and cigars.**

Dining rooms in such households were furnished with the products of the new industrial economy. At Castle Tucker in Wiscasset, Maine, Mollie Tucker's dining room was well supplied with such articles: Britannia pots for tea and coffee, thin porcelain tea sets with colorful floral decoration, an extensive dinner service with 152 pieces of gold-banded porcelain, another everyday service of green-and-pink-banded Davenport porcelain, a breakfast set, a Minton dessert set, polished steel knives and forks, coin-silver teaspoons, and highly ornamented pressed glass in various colors. Many articles were designed for only a single function. Meat, pickle, and butter dishes, lemonade cups, asparagus tongs, knife rests, celery vases, a mustard tureen, eggcups, and a custard stand with twelve covered cups filled the china closet and kitchen pantries of Castle Tucker.

Knowing what to use and when to use it was a challenge for mistress and servants alike. As testimony that the host and hostess were knowledgeable and could afford an extensive and expensive display of food and tablewares, dinner parties became more and more elaborate as the nineteenth century progressed, with many dishes served at each of a large number of courses. Food and decorations were sometimes organized around holidays or other special themes.

Henry Chandler Bowen, who built the Gothic Revival Roseland Cottage in Woodstock, Connecticut, was an abolitionist and a temperance advocate—the personification of Victorian religious and family values. He and his second wife, Ellen Holt, whom he married in 1865, entertained family members, friends, and dignitaries from across the country at dinner parties, picnics, and, most memorable, their Fourth of July celebrations, held annually for twenty-five years, from 1870 to 1895.

At the Bowens'
Fourth of July extrav-
aganzas, guests
enjoyed pink lemon-
ade and cake. In the
evening Japanese
lanterns were lighted,
and a barrage of
fireworks was deto-
nated. President
Benjamin Harrison
(center) was the
guest of honor at the
1889 celebration.

Mid-nineteenth-century wallpaper and furnishings set the tone for the dining room of Sarah Orne Jewett's house in South Berwick, Maine. The fireplace opening has been filled with a wallpaper-covered fire board that prevents birds and insects from flying into the room from the chimney in the summer.

left

Marcia Oakes Woodbury's sepia watercolor "The Sunday Dinner" appeared in the 1893 edition of Sarah Orne Jewett's *Deephaven.* It is based on Jewett's own dining room, which has a similar sideboard placed beneath a painting next to the window.

During the latter part of the nineteenth century, family meals also became increasingly elaborate. Table settings were more formal, and starched white tablecloths and napkins were requisite. At their greenhouses at The Vale, in Waltham, Massachusetts, the Lyman family added cuttings from the famous grapevines at Hampton Court in England and carefully nurtured these to provide fruit for their Thanksgiving table.

In reaction to the formal table settings and social rituals of the Boston elite, Sarah Orne Jewett looked back with affection to the simple old-fashioned rural ways. In her 1877 novel *Deephaven,* she describes in detail the daily activities of a New England village. The 1893 edition contains an illustration entitled "The Sunday Dinner," which recalls the Barrell sisters' breakfast with its clean tablecloth and small amount of food. No floral centerpiece or teacups are evident; instead, the traditional dessert of wine and fruit, with perhaps a bit of cake and a tumbler of water, completes the weekly dinner of the minister and his hostess, his sister, Rebecca Lorimer. In real life, Jewett's friends Emily and Elise Tyson made the Hamilton House in South Berwick, Maine, a center for summer socializing. Their dinner parties featured wholesome, fresh local foods prepared by hired help and elaborate floral table decorations crafted by the hostesses themselves. Like many Victorian women, they also gave afternoon tea parties for women friends and neighbors.

right

Mary Marrett Dudley (left), a member of the Marrett family of Standish, Maine, takes tea with a friend in the parlor of her Nantucket house in 1914. For nearly 150 years, from the late eighteenth century to the early twentieth century, New England's tea ritual changed little.

The Little sisters
entertained friends
and relatives in their
dining room at the
Spencer-Peirce-Little
Farm in Newbury,
Massachusetts. The
room's seventeenth-
century origins are
seen in the exposed
beam and the deep
window seats.

below

Cookbooks from the
kitchens of Historic
New England houses
include (clockwise
from top) *Domestic
Duties or Instructions
for Young Married
Ladies, Mrs. Lincoln's
Boston Cookbook,
American Frugal
Housewife, Miss
Parloa's New Cook-
book,* and *Cook's
Oracle and House-
keeper Manual.*

New England led the way at the end of the nineteenth century in formulating and popularizing a more rigorous approach to domestic economy based on scientific principles. Known as home economics or domestic science, the movement was centered around the Boston Cooking-School, founded in 1879 by the Women's Education Association and the cookbook author Maria Parloa. In her many publications, Parloa assured women that their status as household managers would be enhanced if they understood nutrition, digestion, combustion, and the components of a balanced diet. *Miss Parloa's New Cookbook: A Guide to Marketing and Cooking* (1881), a well-worn copy of which is at Castle Tucker, illustrates useful and necessary cooking equipment, much of which was owned and used by Mollie Tucker and her daughter Jane. Another cookbook at Castle Tucker that also derives from the Boston Cooking-School is *Mrs. Lincoln's Boston Cookbook: What to Do and What Not to Do* (1892), which contains recipes for quantity cooking and food suitable for invalids and children as well as suggested menus for family dinners for each season of the year.

For some women, education in household science took them out of the home and into the work force. Such was the case with Amelia Little, one of the last family members to live at the Spencer-Peirce-Little Farm in Newbury, Massachusetts. After studying cookery, marketing, and household management as well as chemistry, biology, and bacteriology at Simmons College in Boston in 1912–13, she served as the dietician at the nearby Groton School until her retirement in the 1950s, returning to the farm each summer. There she and her sisters and cousin took pride in serving homemade bread as well as fresh and preserved products of their farm at parties and meetings of their reading club. At the fortieth anniversary luncheon of their reading club, the members enjoyed "a vast platter laden with slices of cold chicken and ham and at strategic places along the table were placed dishes of green beans, tossed salad, and blueberry muffins, all up to the usual farm standard.... Dessert was deep red raspberries surrounding a mound of cottage cheese (Amelia's speciality) with cream to add if one wished and— Agnes['s] chef d'oeuvre—a magnificent birthday cake."

For all the new scientific attention to nutrition and the labor-saving convenience of processed foods and new appliances, it was the attractive presentation of delicious food that received the greatest acclaim. Few new homes were built without dining rooms, and at least one had several. At Beauport in Gloucester, Massachusetts, Henry Sleeper designed and had built a central kitchen with service pantries radiating out to five dining rooms, each with its own theme and suited for a specific type of food. Old-fashioned New England fare was served up on thick redware plates in the Pine Kitchen; in other rooms the food and decorations were maritime, medieval, Chinese, or French. Sleeper instructed his cook, Mary Wonson, not to skimp, so meals at Beauport were renowned for their fresh ingredients and lavish use of lobster, wild rice, butter, and cream, as well as for their dramatic settings and efficient service.

The Gropiuses created a study in black and white in the dining room of their house in Lincoln, Massachusetts. The spotlight on the round white table set with black plates provided a dramatic effect during dinner parties. The Gropiuses brought with them to the new house the table and tubular steel chairs with canvas coverings. Designed by Marcel Breuer, they were made around 1925 in the Bauhaus workshops, where Gropius was director.

At the boldly modern home of the Bauhaus architect Walter Gropius in Lincoln, Massachusetts, the conversation and design of the dining room eclipsed the food itself. The round white table was lighted by a spotlight, originally designed for a theater, that created dramatic shadows, cast a flattering reflected light on the guests' faces, and kept the rest of the room dark. The walls seemed to disappear as the floodlighted landscape filled the floor-to-ceiling windows. Usually only one other couple was invited to dinner, and long before the invention of *nouvelle cuisine* the black dinner plates featured an artful arrangement of perhaps one cherry tomato, a few perfectly positioned green beans, and some elegantly sliced pieces of meat or a bit of fish.

No matter how artfully displayed or how complex and ethnically diverse New England cuisine has become in the last fifty years, long-time traditions and distinctive regional specialties are still celebrated annually on Thanksgiving, as they have been for hundreds of years. In search of the quintessential New England Thanksgiving, *McCall's* magazine sent a writer and photographer to the coastal village of Wiscasset, Maine, to share dinner with four generations of the Sortwell family at the Nickels-Sortwell House. The resulting article, which appeared in the November 1949 issue, included recipes for two menus. One began with oysters on the half shell and the other with creamed lobster in patty shells, but both featured roast turkey with stuffing, gravy, an assortment of vegetables, rolls, pickles, and two desserts. *McCall's* summed up the celebration:

Thanksgiving dinner at the Sortwells' in Wiscasset, Maine

Hardly an American old enough to vote, we'd guess, who doesn't think of Thanksgiving in terms of the old New England Thanksgiving. The bright, shiny November day, the damask covered table heavy with the good fruits of the land, the fine old house rich in tradition and beauty.... For nearly 150 years, on each Thanksgiving day this lovely room has been the scene of a great feast. Men, women, and children giving thanks for the blessings of this great land. It is the American tradition at its best, the tradition we should all cherish and remember.

left

In 1949 *McCall's* magazine shared with readers the Sortwell family's annual Thanksgiving gathering at the Nickels-Sortwell House in Wiscasset, Maine.

REMEMBERING THE PAST

"How the people of those remote days lived, how they fared, what their mode of life, their methods of household furniture and supplies, are matters of deep interest to us—if, in nothing else, at least in the contrast of their simplicity and plainness with our artificial methods and manners . . . the day of the shoddy not having dawned either in men or things."

Boston Daily Advertiser, December 16, 1875

Pages 192–93

The writer Sarah Orne Jewett was photographed in midcareer at her desk in her South Berwick, Maine, home. Her novels and short stories testify to her reverence for old New England.

Acknowledging the interest in New England antiquities that had blossomed by 1875, the *Boston Daily Advertiser* described an exhibition of "very interesting old articles" assembled by the Ladies' Centennial Committee and held at the Essex Institute in Salem, Massachusetts. The exhibition's "bewildering superfluity" of authentic articles was intended to evoke admiration and respect for "the era of hard courage and self-sacrifice," those earlier times so different from the modern world. A year later, New England's special place in American history took center stage nationally with the 1876 Centennial Exhibition in Philadelphia. As the several million visitors marveled at the accomplishments of the machine age, they also stepped into the "New England Kitchen" to view antique furnishings and domestic implements associated with prominent families and arranged to reinforce ideas about the virtues and accomplishments of early settlers. In turn, the centennial inspired more local exhibitions, costumed pageants, and Lady Washington tea parties. This memorialization of old New England—objects, places, activities, people, and values, both public and private—continues to this day.

The work of the earliest New England preservationists—the people who kept alive traditions and memories—was selective. A few individuals in each community and in some families remembered the past, identified important places and objects, wrote down details, knew which portrait was of whom, recovered family heirlooms, and told the stories that imbued particular objects and places with historical significance. For memory to live, one generation had to tell the next about the things that mattered.

opposite

Bertram and Nina Fletcher Little expressed their understanding of early New England art and culture in the way they furnished Cogswell's Grant, their summer home in Essex, Massachusetts.

left

Lucy Coffin lived at the Coffin House in Newbury, Massachusetts throughout her long life, from 1811 until 1893. In 1929 Coffin family descendants donated the house to Historic New England in response to Edmund Coffin Coleman's testamentary request "to memorialize our revered parents in some worthy manner."

The 1735 centennial of Newbury, Massachusetts, was celebrated "in the front yard of the old Coffin House, under the shade of a lofty elm, remarkable for its great size and graceful shape." By this time members of the Coffin family had already lived in their house on High Road for fifty-seven years. Theirs was not the oldest house in town, but the current patriarch, Nathaniel Coffin, was a prominent member of the community—like his father, Tristram Jr., he was a selectman and a deacon—and his house's proximity to the meetinghouse made the location convenient and symbolically important. More than a hundred years later, in a small room in the same house, Joshua Coffin wrote the history of the town of Newbury. In 1929 the Coffin House and many of the family furnishings were given to Historic New England.

During its more than three-hundred-year history in Massachusetts, the Coffin family has acted on preservation impulses: the commemoration of people and places, a passion for written narrative and definition of detail, and creation of a shrine to one's family as a focal point. Like many other historic houses in New England, the Coffin House and the family heirlooms so carefully arranged within it are a physical expression of cultural memory, a three-dimensional textbook in which one can read many stories. Not surprisingly, its stories are far more varied than those that were important to the donor, Edmund Coffin Coleman. Each generation brings its own experience to the study of history, deriving different meanings from architectural forms, the selection and arrangement of objects, the written record, and the oral history preserved together in such a place.

far left

At this desk in a tiny room in the family homestead, Joshua Coffin wrote his *Sketch of the History of Newbury, Newburyport, and West Newbury,* covering the years from 1635 to 1845.

Even before the American Revolution, Jonathan Sayward used his home in York Harbor, Maine, and certain possessions to convey to his community and descendants the significance of historical events and the importance of family. In his own large portrait that hangs in the parlor is evidence of his occupation as a coastal and West Indies trader. Next to it hangs a coat of arms painted by John Gore, a New England artist, and intended to convey the family's social status and historical importance. To enhance the family's social position well into the future, Sayward's widow and descendants were governed by a provision in his will specifying that the "clock, a large Map of North America, the Family and other Pictures are to be taken and considered as appurtenant to my Mansion House." As a result, the parlor remains almost unchanged to this day.

As early as 1869 Jonathan Sayward's great-granddaughters Elizabeth and Mary Barrell opened their home to visitors and took pride in showing the "great number of articles worth the attention of those of historical, antiquarian taste." The writer Sarah Orne Jewett knew these two elderly women well, and she likely had them in mind when she wrote of people who embodied "all the individuality and quaint personal characteristics of rural New England." Many of their generation who remained in New England villages were those daughters left behind when brothers and married sisters moved away or those whose sweethearts had fought in the Civil War and never returned. Trapped by poverty and circumstance, these women were often proud and fiercely defensive of the old things and old ways. Using their inherited possessions to define a genteel status for themselves, they resisted selling family heirlooms and even accepted paying guests.

below

Judge Jonathan Sayward, a successful merchant and ship owner, decreed that his portrait remain in his house in York Harbor, Maine. It now reminds visitors of his worldly success and authority.

right

Posing at their home in 1880, Elizabeth and Mary Barrell wore dresses from two decades earlier—a sign of their frugality. Their house was "as fresh as white paint can make it," said a reporter in 1878.

All around them, New England was changing. Despite the establishment of water-powered textile and woodworking mills in small towns, the region had lost population since the Erie Canal opened up an easy path to the fertile lands of the old Northwest Territory. In addition, the lure of industrial wages and urban life proved irresistible to many women as well as men. At the end of the century immigrants were arriving from Mediterranean and eastern European countries, and the pace of change was accelerating. The old quiet rural way of life was no longer part of many Americans' experience. Even in South Berwick, Maine, Sarah Orne Jewett's hometown, the shops were stocked with manufactured goods, and the noise of the mill permeated the village. Yet, many people cherished an image of a New England as a timeless place, the birthplace of America and American ideals. Some people began looking at old things in a new way.

In Quincy, Massachusetts, Eliza Susan Quincy began gathering family heirlooms in the 1840s, inventoried the contents of her family home in 1879, and commissioned

photographs of the first-floor rooms the following year. When the Lyman family decided to move to The Vale in Waltham, Massachusetts, for year-round living after the death of Arthur Lyman in 1884, they made many changes to the house, but they left the original architectural form and the furnishings of the bow parlor intact; they only changed the wallpaper and added straw matting. Ralph May and his mother were so successful at retrieving family heirlooms in the 1920s that they ultimately combined many of the original furnishings of two early-nineteenth-century Portsmouth, New Hampshire, households at the Rundlet-May House, thus making it appear to have been much more lavishly furnished than it actually was in 1808. In Lincoln, Massachusetts, the siblings Ogden Jr., Tom, and Dorothy Codman pursued the same course, doubling the number of paintings that had belonged to their great-great-uncle Richard Codman and their mother's family, the Bradlees. They hung all these paintings at The Grange in Lincoln, enhancing the interior while making what amounts to an overstatement about their ancestors' taste and prosperity.

above

Ella Lowell Lyman noted in her diary that "we decided against altering the bow parlor" of The Vale in Waltham, Massachusetts, despite making other changes in the 1880s. "We cannot bear to touch it . . . for it is the only room except the library as it was."

left

Emily Tyson and Sarah Orne Jewett stand in the garden pergola of the Hamilton House in 1905. A fellow resident of South Berwick, Maine, Jewett had long kept watch over this historic house.

opposite

The stately elms, the soaring eagle, and the millstone in the garden path at the Hamilton House in the 1920s evoked tradition, patriotism, and hard work—important concepts to proponents of the Colonial Revival style.

When Emily and Elise Tyson purchased the Hamilton House in South Berwick, Maine, in 1898 and set about creating a superior expression of the Colonial Revival style, they relied on the contemporary fondness for the colonial period and on oral tradition rather than documentary research. The Tysons carefully reproduced the original wallpaper in the stair hall but exhibited great creativity in other rooms. For the double drawing room they chose to illustrate in murals the historic buildings of the Piscataqua region of Maine and New Hampshire—a variation of the popular French wallpaper called the "Monuments of Paris," and for the dining room they chose scenes of Italian gardens. They did not use family heirlooms but purchased a variety of antiques dating from the seventeenth to the end of the nineteenth century to convey the house's history. The rigors of New England's climate are depicted in lithographs of winter scenes by Currier and Ives, while Jonathan Hamilton's trade—he was a merchant whose wharves and warehouses once occupied the riverbank below the house—is reflected in ship models, Chinese objects, maritime prints, and hooked rugs depicting ships. Sequestering the kitchen and bathrooms in newly added wings and moving the barn away from the site of the new garden enhanced the romantic effect by keeping the bustle and smell of everyday activities out of the way.

The garden cottage at the Hamilton House, added in the summer of 1907, provided a romantic retreat at the far side of the garden. Inside, it was paneled with wood salvaged from the Sally Hart House (ca. 1740) in Newington, New Hampshire.

far right

In 1907 George Porter Fernald painted over the recently installed wallpaper in the parlor at the Hamilton House, creating a romantic mural of historic houses and other points of interest in the area.

right below

Elise Tyson (center) used the dining room to entertain friends at tea in 1903. The combination of painted "Boston" chairs, an Empire-style table, and shaded Edwardian candlesticks typify Colonial Revival eclecticism.

right

The dilapidated house of William Cogswell in Essex, Massachusetts, constructed in the early eighteenth century, caught the eye of Henry Sleeper and the great Boston collector Isabella Stewart Gardner as they drove north to visit the Hamilton House in September 1907. They returned another day, thoroughly explored the house, and rescued some architectural elements from it.

below

Henry Sleeper, who posed for an oil portrait by the artist Wallace Bryant in 1906, loved to entertain. His personal charisma and Beauport's fantastic settings ensured his success as a host.

The Hamilton House's influence on home decoration and garden design was far-reaching. Visitors took away ideas for their own houses, and others drew inspiration from the four illustrated articles about it published in *House Beautiful* in 1929. Some people exactly copied details from the Hamilton House, while others adapted them for their own creations. Such was the case with Henry Davis Sleeper, who visited the Hamilton House in 1907, when he was beginning to develop Beauport, his summer house on Eastern Point in Gloucester, Massachusetts. Inspired by the Tysons' rooms and their installation of early-eighteenth-century paneling in the new garden cottage, Sleeper purchased antique paneling from the Cogswell House (not Cogswell's Grant, but nearby) in Essex, Massachusetts, and began the synchronous arrangements of color and the thematic installations of associative objects that still characterize Beauport. Drawing inspiration also from nearby Indian Hill in West Newbury and historic sites in Virginia, Sleeper enlarged his house over two decades, creating more than forty rooms that were at once expressive of historical and literary themes and suitable for his expansive entertaining style. Beginning in 1916, this house, too, had been featured in *House Beautiful* and other magazines, spreading images of Sleeper's "truly American" taste far and wide.

opposite

Sleeper installed paneling from the Cogswell House in the Green Dining Room at Beauport in Gloucester, Massachusetts. The color was one of the "seven colonial colors" that he promoted.

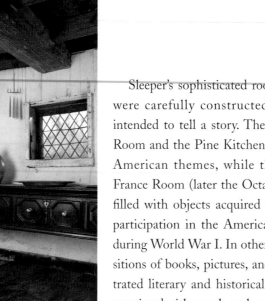

Sleeper's sophisticated rooms at Beauport were carefully constructed arrangements intended to tell a story. The Franklin Game Room and the Pine Kitchen commemorated American themes, while the Souvenir de France Room (later the Octagon Room) was filled with objects acquired during Sleeper's participation in the American Field Service during World War I. In other rooms juxtapositions of books, pictures, and ceramics illustrated literary and historical themes; objects associated with people such as Lord Byron and Horace Walpole were clustered together. When Helena Woolworth McCann acquired Beauport in 1935 after Sleeper's death, she made major changes to only one room, the China Trade Room. After her death her children, Constance McCann Betts, Frasier W. McCann, and Helena W. McCann Guest, respecting her wishes, made no further changes until they presented Beauport, largely intact, to Historic New England in 1946.

Another antiquarian who created rooms with similar themes was William Perry Dudley, who exposed seventeenth-century interior details of the Gilman Garrison House in Exeter, New Hampshire, built about 1690, to underscore its early date and "tell stories of stalwart defense against the Indians." In the eighteenth-century portion of the house he furnished one room, which he called the Council Chamber, to depict the story of "the creation of an independent government."

above and right

At the Gilman Garrison House in Exeter, New Hampshire, the Puncheon Floor Room (above) recalls the house's seventeenth-century origins. In the Council Chamber (right), William Perry Dudley sought to re-create the Revolutionary days when the colony's Governor's Council may have met here.

opposite bottom

Sleeper added his Souvenir de France Room to Beauport in 1920–21, after he returned from France. Lafayette's portrait is featured along with French toiles and toleware that harmonize with the red leather book bindings. The space was later renamed the Octagon Room.

The passion for collecting New England antiques reached new heights in the 1920s. Many collectors mixed objects from several historical periods, prizing the oldest most highly. Evidence of handcraftsmanship was especially valued, and collectors often stripped original paint from furniture and historic paneling to emphasize the marks of hand tools. Mary Thacher, an active collector in this tradition, bought and preserved the Winslow Crocker House in Yarmouth Port, Massachusetts, built about 1780, as a suitable setting for her re-creation of an early New England home. To enhance its credibility as a distinguished eighteenth-century house, she brought together a few family furnishings, collected many more of the period, and even moved the house so that it would be in a better part of town.

The guest room at Cogswell's Grant reflects the Littles' collecting and research interests: New England folk painting, early painted furniture, decoys, maritime objects, lighting devices, rugs, and anything else that was unusual, quirky, or amusing.

A quite different approach to collecting was that pursued by Bertram K. and Nina Fletcher Little, both dedicated students of New England architecture and artifacts. As director of Historic New England from William Sumner Appleton's death in 1947 to his own retirement in 1970, Bert Little was particularly interested in architecture and historic preservation. His wife pursued a variety of research topics and published more than 150 articles and books, particularly in the field of folk art; she was the first to identify the work of many New England portrait painters and other artists. Their summer home, Cogswell's Grant in Essex, Massachusetts, mirrors the course of their research and contains superb examples of the many objects that interested them over the years, almost every one reflecting the Littles' quest for the story of its original maker, ownership, and use. The selection and placement of these objects in the rooms at Cogswell's Grant were never intended to re-create actual eighteenth-century interiors but were governed by sophisticated attention to color and form, the intrinsic relationships of objects to one another, the Littles' definition of what was suitable for an eighteenth-century New England farmhouse, and the needs of comfortable summer living for their family and friends.

right

In Nina Fletcher Little's tiny office at Cogswell's Grant in Essex, Massachusetts, she catalogued her collections, kept farm accounts, and pursued a voluminous correspondence with students, collectors, and antiques dealers. Favorite decoys and research books fill the shelves.

opposite bottom

As Sarah Orne Jewett described a typical New England attic in *Deephaven*, the Littles' attic was a place where "nothing seems to have been thrown away." Treasured boxes range from a rare seventeenth-century blanket chest (left), heavily used but never restored, to an unused coffin (right).

Since these owners began to save their own memories of New England, approaches to preservation and the interpretation of historic places have changed. Historic New England's own goal in the past century, as it continues the work of these earlier preservationists, has always been to preserve its historic properties for research and enjoyment now and in the future. William Sumner Appleton was particularly interested in showing a building's original appearance and saving as much of the original materials as possible, but he was not averse to aggressive restoration—that is, reproducing lost architectural elements, wallpaper, furnishing schemes, and decorative treatments to fill out the picture and achieve the desired effect. His decisions were based on meticulous scholarship and carefully documented with photographs and written notes. Historic New England's most ambitious restoration project during his tenure was the 1698 Browne House in Watertown, Massachusetts.

The Victorian-era parlor at the Spencer-Peirce-Little House in Newbury, Massachusetts, shows how the Little family lived about 1870. The patterned wallpaper and carpet, the green table covering and curtains, and the furniture arrangement are typical of the day.

Although they preserved Beauport intact, Appleton's successors, Bertram Little and Abbott Lowell Cummings, undertook aggressive restoration of earlier houses, carefully documenting their work in removing Victorian porches at the Casey Farm in Saunderstown, Rhode Island; taking down the wings that housed Emily Tyson's kitchen and sleeping porches at the Hamilton House in South Berwick, Maine; exposing the stone end and replacing the casement windows at the Arnold House in Lincoln, Rhode Island, built in 1693, and meticulously re-creating the first wallpapers, original paint colors, and an appropriate furnishing plan for the Otis House in Boston. The impulse to replicate the original appearance of houses was largely abandoned, however, as Historic New England became the owner of several properties with thousands of family objects assembled over many generations and decorative schemes that illustrated change through the years. Now, consistently using a more comprehensive approach to preservation, the organization's goal is to preserve the property as it was when it was acquired rather than to aggressively restore it to some earlier moment in the past.

Historic New England's acquisition of its first Victorian building complex, the 1846 Roseland Cottage in Woodstock, Connecticut, together with many of its original family furnishings and a rich accumulation of nineteenth-century material, opened the door for conversations and negotiations with Ise Gropius, the widow of Walter Gropius. Their twentieth-century landmark, completed in 1938, soon came under Historic New England's umbrella, along with all of its furnishings, art, and personal effects. Such properties represent many layers of history and offer multiple interpretations, proving that the pool of things worth saving is much broader than the colonial.

Each generation's perception of the past is filtered through its own experience, its memories, and the preservation activities of those who have come before—by people such as Elizabeth and Mary Barrell in York Harbor, Maine, who kept their great-grandfather's house sacrosanct; Sarah Orne Jewett, who penned an indelible impression of New England; and the many self-appointed family historians and owners who have tried to reflect the past in their homes. Yet evidence of old ways and old values remains reassuring. Those things that served New Englanders well in the face of earlier hardships offer continuing hope for coping with the complexities of contemporary life and the accelerating pace of social change.

right

Because Ise Gropius donated even her coats and hats when she conveyed her modern house in Lincoln, Massachusetts, to Historic New England, visitors are able to gain a complete picture of how the Bauhaus founder and his wife lived in their home.

𝒫RIVATE OWNERSHIP, PERMANENT PROTECTION

"In the past the only way to guarantee permanent protection of one's property was to donate it to some organization as a house museum. But in today's economy few can afford to do that. Realizing this, the Society for the Preservation of New England Antiquities, the nation's largest regional preservation organization, has come up with an affordable alternative. It's called the Stewardship Program."

Boston Sunday Globe, May 9, 1982

Plagued with mounting maintenance costs, inadequate endowments, and the desire to find the best uses for historic buildings that were not being fully used as house museums, the Society for the Preservation of New England Antiquities (now Historic New England) made a decision in 1980 that dramatically changed the way owners in New England view the future of their historic homes.

That year, four of the organization's properties—the Fowler House (1809) in Danvers, Massachusetts; the Short House (ca. 1732) in Newbury, Massachusetts; the Merrell Tavern (ca. 1790) in South Lee, Massachusetts; and the Sanford-Covell House (1870) in Newport, Rhode Island—were sold and returned to private ownership. This step led to the creation of one of the earliest, most comprehensive preservation easement programs in the country. Today the program has grown to protect more than seventy-five historic properties throughout New England that date from the seventeenth to the twentieth centuries.

Historic New England's Stewardship Program was established on April 29, 1981, as a practical, permanent way to ensure the preservation of privately owned historic buildings and landscapes while keeping them in active use. This goal is accomplished through a preservation easement, a perpetual legal agreement that is recorded in local land records. By donating a preservation easement, a property owner transfers certain rights to Historic New England, entrusting the organization to protect the property's historic features from inappropriate alteration, demolition, or neglect. In this partnership, Historic New England's experts work with a property owner to monitor a historic property, review proposed plans for building or landscape alterations, and ensure that any change or maintenance work is done sensitively and does not damage the historic features of the protected building or landscape.

pages 216–17

Merrell Tavern in South Lee, Massachusetts, which operates as an inn today, is one of four properties that were returned to private ownership to create the Historic New England Stewardship Program.

far left

The eighteenth-century wood paneling in the parlor of the Norwood-Hyatt House (ca. 1664) in Gloucester, Massachusetts, was allegedly found in outbuildings on the property and reinstalled in the early 1900s.

left

The painted wood graining on parlor doors of the Sampson-Gifford House (1804) in Duxbury, Massachusetts, is protected by preservation easements.

right top

right top

Now owned by the Townsend (Massachusetts) Historical Society, the Spaulding Cooperage (ca. 1845), located on the Squannacook River, historically operated as a cooperage for barrel making.

far right

From 1868 until 1989, the Griffin family operated a potato farm in Caribou, Maine. The Historic New England Stewardship Program protects one hundred acres at Griffin Farm as well as this early-twentieth-century farmhouse.

right below

The Stewardship Program easements encompass the stone walls and open fields at Jacobs Farm, in Norwell, Massachusetts. The property is owned by the town and continues to be actively farmed.

Although preservation easements were already being used in the 1980s in places such as California, Illinois, Maryland, New York, and Virginia, the Historic New England Stewardship Program is one of the region's oldest holders of preservation easements. What sets its program apart is the extent of its coverage. It is one of the few programs that protect not just exterior architectural features, but also interior details and finishes, such as staircases, fireplaces, moldings, hardware, historic wallpaper, and decorative painting. Landscape features, such as stone walls and fences, and outbuildings, such as barns and garages, are also protected. Subdivision of the land is prohibited to preserve a property's context and views.

Features protected through a preservation easement are tailored to each historic property's significance and evolution. After receiving an application, Historic New England staff conduct an initial site visit to inspect the property and begin the process of identifying the architectural and landscape features to be covered. Documentary photographs are taken to supplement written descriptions of protected features. Once the owner and Historic New England agree on the details, the easement document is written, signed, and recorded. A preservation easement is legally binding on all future owners. If a property changes hands, the easement remains in place and Historic New England continues to ensure protection.

At the Sanford-Covell
House (1870) in
Newport, Rhode
Island, the impressive
stair hall, shown here
before interior
restoration work in
1986, rises thirty-five
feet from floor
to ceiling. The floors
are made from six
species of wood.

The original lighting
fixtures, intricate
stenciling, and three-
story staircase at the
Sanford-Covell House
are all protected
under Historic New
England's Steward-
ship Program.

When Historic New England launched the Stewardship Program, it put preservation easements on the four properties it sold to ensure their longevity. Proceeds from the sales were designated to establish the Stewardship Fund, an endowment that generates revenue to support the program's operations. Owners who enter their properties into the Stewardship Program are asked to make endowment contributions that support the administration of the preservation easements. The endowment contribution may be paid in full at the time an easement is recorded, in installments, or from the proceeds of the property's sale.

In the initial proposal for creation of the Stewardship Program, forward-thinking staff wrote a statement that remains true today:

Few organizations are as capable of establishing an effective regional program of acquiring preservation restrictions. [Our] corporate goal is to protect and preserve buildings and objects of historical import throughout New England, and the organization is well known and has the support of a large membership. The staff has the necessary expertise to identify the features needing protection in important structures, to instruct property owners in the best means of building conservation, and to enforce detailed preservation restrictions.

For more information on the Historic New England Stewardship Program, visit www.HistoricNewEngland.org.

left

The Hoover House and its landscape in Lincoln, Massachusetts, were designed to take full advantage of sweeping views of the nearby Cambridge Reservoir.

below

A 2008 addition to the Stewardship Program, the Hoover House was built in 1937 by the architect Henry B. Hoover for his family. Hoover himself enlarged the house in 1955 by adding a bedroom wing and a carport.

Arnold House

1693

487 Great Road

Lincoln, R.I. 02865

Boardman House

1692

17 Howard Street

Saugus, Mass. 01906

Barrett House

(Forest Hall)

ca. 1800

79 Main Street

New Ipswich, N.H.

03071

Browne House

ca. 1698

562 Main Street

Watertown, Mass.

02172

Beauport (Sleeper-

McCann House)

1907–34

75 Eastern Point

Boulevard

Gloucester, Mass.

01930

Casey Farm

ca. 1750

2325 Boston Neck

Road

Saunderstown, R.I.

02874

Castle Tucker
1807
2 Lee Street
Wiscasset, Maine
04578

Coffin House
1678
14 High Road
(Route 1A)
Newbury, Mass.
01951

Clemence-Irons
House
1691
38 George Waterman
Road
Johnston, R.I. 02919

Cogswell's Grant
1728
60 Spring Street
Essex, Mass. 01929

Codman Estate
(The Grange)
ca. 1740
34 Codman Road
Lincoln, Mass. 01773

Cooper-Frost-Austin
House
1681
21 Linnaean Street
Cambridge, Mass.
02138

Winslow Crocker
House
ca. 1780
250 Main Street
(Old King's Highway)
Yarmouth Port, Mass.
02675

Gilman Garrison
House
1709
12 Water Street
Exeter, N.H. 03833

Dole-Little House
ca. 1715
289 High Road
Newbury, Mass.
01951

Gropius House
1938
68 Baker Bridge Road
Lincoln, Mass. 01773

Gedney House
1665
21 High Street
Salem, Mass. 01970

Hamilton House
ca. 1785
40 Vaughan's Lane
South Berwick, Maine
03908

Jackson House
ca. 1664
76 Northwest Street
Portsmouth, N.H.
03801

Lyman Estate
(The Vale)
1793
185 Lyman Street
Waltham, Mass.
02452

Sarah Orne Jewett
House
1774
5 Portland Street
South Berwick, Maine
03908

Marrett House
1789
Route 25
Standish, Maine
04084

Governor John
Langdon House
1784
143 Pleasant Street
Portsmouth, N.H.
03801

Merwin House
(Tranquility)
ca. 1825
14 Main Street
Stockbridge, Mass.
01262

Nickels-Sortwell
House
1807
121 Main Street
Wiscasset, Maine
04578

Pierce House
1683
24 Oakton Avenue
Dorchester, Mass.
02122

Harrison Gray Otis
House
1796
141 Cambridge Street
Boston, Mass. 02114

Quincy House
1770
20 Muirhead Street
Quincy, Mass. 02170

Phillips House
1821
34 Chestnut Street
Salem, Mass. 01970

Rocky Hill Meeting
House
1785
4 Portsmouth Road
Amesbury, Mass.
01913

Roseland Cottage
1846
556 Route 169
Woodstock, Conn.
06281

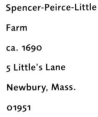

Spencer-Peirce-Little
Farm
ca. 1690
5 Little's Lane
Newbury, Mass.
01951

Rundlet-May House
1807
364 Middle Street
Portsmouth, N.H.
03801

Swett-Ilsley House
ca. 1670
4 High Road
Newbury, Mass.
01951

Sayward-Wheeler
House
ca. 1718
9 Barrell Lane
Extension
York Harbor, Maine
03911

Watson Farm
1796
455 North Road
Jamestown, R.I.
02835

House museums are open June 1–October 15 or year-round.

For more information, visit Historic New England's web site at www.HistoricNewEngland.org.

Blackburn, Roderic H., and Geoffrey Gross. *Great Houses of New England.* New York: Rizzoli, 2008.

Blanchard, Paula. *Sarah Orne Jewett: Her World and Her Work.* Reading, Mass.: Addison-Wesley, 1994.

Carlisle, Nancy. *Cherished Possessions: A New England Legacy.* Boston: Society for the Preservation of New England Antiquities, 2003.

Carlisle, Nancy, and Melinda Talbot Nasardinov. *America's Kitchens.* Boston: Historic New England, 2008.

"The Codman Estate." Edited by Abbott Lowell Cummings. *Old-Time New England* 71, no. 258 (1981).

Cowan, Ruth Schwartz. *More Work for Mother: The Ironies of Household Technology from the Open Hearth to the Microwave.* New York: Basic Books, 1983.

Cummings, Abbott Lowell. *Architecture in Early New England.* 1958. Rev. ed. Sturbridge, Mass.: Old Sturbridge Village, 1984.

Curtis, Nancy, and Richard C. Nylander. *Beauport.* Historic New England. Boston: David R. Godine, 1990.

Downing, Andrew Jackson. *The Architecture of Country Houses.* 1859. Reprint, New York: Dover Publications, 1969.

Emmet, Alan. *So Fine a Prospect: Historic New England Gardens.* Hanover, N.H.: University Press of New England, 1996.

Giffen, Sarah L., and Kevin D. Murphy, eds. *A Noble and Dignified Stream: The Piscataqua Region in the Colonial Revival.* York, Maine: Old York Historical Society, 1992.

Gropius, Ise. *Gropius House: A History by Ise Gropius.* Boston: Historic New England, 1977.

Handlin, David P. *The American Home: Architecture and Society, 1815–1915.* Boston: Little, Brown, 1979.

Hosmer, Charles B., Jr. *Presence of the Past: A History of the Preservation Movement in the United States Before Williamsburg.* New York: Putnam, 1965.

————. *Preservation Comes of Age: From Williamsburg to the National Trust, 1926–1949.* 2 vols. Preservation Press, National Trust for Historic Preservation. Charlottesville: University Press of Virginia, 1981.

Isaacs, Reginald. *Gropius: An Illustrated Biography of the Creator of the Bauhaus.* Boston: Bulfinch Press, 1991.

Jewett, Sarah Orne. *Deephaven.* 1877. Reprint, Portsmouth, N.H.: Peter E. Randall, Old Berwick Historical Society, 1993.

Lindgren, James M. *Preserving Historic New England: Preservation, Progressivism, and the Remaking of Memory.* New York: Oxford University Press, 1995.

Little, Nina Fletcher. *Country Arts in Early American Homes.* 1975. Rev. ed. Boston: Historic New England, 1999.

————. *Little by Little: Six Decades of Collecting American Decorative Arts.* 1984. Rev. ed. Boston: Historic New England, 1998.

Morison, Samuel Eliot. *Harrison Gray Otis, 1765–1848: The Urbane Federalist.* Boston: Houghton Mifflin, 1969.

Nylander, Jane C. *Our Own Snug Fireside: Images of the New England Home, 1760-1860.* New Haven, Conn.: Yale University Press, 1983.

Roberts, Robert. *The House Servant's Directory.* 1827. Reprint, Armonk, N.Y.: M. E. Sharpe, 1998.

Stein, Roger B., and William H. Truettner, eds. *Picturing Old New England: Image and Memory.* National Museum of American Art, Smithsonian Institution. New Haven, Conn.: Yale University Press, 1999.

Williams, Susan. *Savory Suppers and Fashionable Feasts: Dining in Victorian America.* New York: Pantheon Books, 1985.

Like many books, *Windows on the Past* represents the inspiration and collaboration of many people, none more important than those who created and cherished homes in the historic houses now belonging to the Society for the Preservation of New England Antiquities. Through four centuries these New Englanders worked their land, built their houses, redecorated their interiors, rearranged their furniture, displayed their keepsakes, and preserved the things that now make up SPNEA's extraordinarily rich collection. We are indebted to all of them for preserving these treasures and placing them in our hands.

As it illustrates these treasures and earlier lifestyles, the book also reflects the talent and commitment of the SPNEA staff through the years: the discerning collecting and fine scholarship of William Sumner Appleton, Bertram K. Little, and Abbott Lowell Cummings, as well as the responsible stewardship of Nancy Coolidge and all those who have served SPNEA as trustees. We are especially grateful to the current trustees and notably Robert Owens, chair, for their support of this project.

The book's original concept and organizing themes were developed by Kenneth Ames, who unfortunately was unable to complete the project. As coauthors, we have worked closely with a staff publication committee that has suggested themes and illustration topics, provided research information, and reviewed text. We thank each of them: Nancy Carlisle, Peter Gittleman, Anne Grady, and Richard Nylander. Other Historic New England staff members who were especially helpful include Rebecca Aaronson, Kathi Gellar, Betsy Igleheart, Melinda Linderer, Laura Roberts, Jennifer Swope, John Tarvin, and Bill Tramposch. The assistance of Lorna Condon, archivist and publication committee member, was invaluable, and Joan Kertis provided important additional support.

The book owes much to Diane Maddex of Archetype Press, whose idea it was to publish it; to Gretchen Smith Mui, editor; and to Robert L. Wiser, designer. We appreciate the many ways in which they have brought clarity to our work and improved its appearance. Any faults in the text, however, remain entirely our own.

The glory of this book is certainly its photographs, and for those we thank David Bohl, who was Historic New England's photographer for twenty-three years. Drawing on his long experience in observing these properties, he took seriously our charge to show them in ways never seen before. He capitalized on dawn's early light and twilight's last hour, enjoyed glorious summer days, and undertook many hasty drives to catch a view before fresh snow was marred or melted. For his talent and determination to make this a beautiful book, we are indeed grateful. Our contribution pales next to his.

Writing as coauthors is often not an easy task, but we have found harmony in our perceptions of the way to share ideas and images. Further, we have found loving support at home, and for that we wish to thank Tom Giffen, Sarah Rooker, Carl and Gary Viera, and Timothy and Richard Nylander.

Jane C. Nylander and Diane L. Viera

It is hard to believe that a decade has passed since the first edition of *Windows on the Past* was published. As is the case in life, much has changed, but many important things remain constant. One of the constants that will always be a cornerstone of Historic New England (as the Society for the Preservation of New England Antiquities was renamed in 2004) is the dedicated staff. I continue to be indebted to them for an unwavering commitment to caring for and sharing the organization's unparalleled collection of properties, objects and stories.

Much gratitude is also due the generous donors whose support allows us to bring the region's history to life. I am especially grateful to the Historic New England trustees for their dedication, including Chairman William C. S. Hicks, who supported this project in so many ways.

Long-time friends of Historic New England will find new information in these pages. I am grateful to the researchers who come to us with a passion for their subject and make us a better institution because of their work. For their wealth of knowledge and belief that there is always more to discover, I thank Margherita Desy, Merrill Kohlhofer, Jennifer Pustz, and Linda Shoemaker. I am also sincerely grateful to Julie Arrison, Lorna Condon, Joseph Cornish, Nancy Curtis, Jeanne Gamble, Pilar Garro, Peter Gittleman, Peggy Konitzky, Megan MacNeil, Wendy Price, Kathleen Simone, Ken Turino, and other colleagues who willingly stepped beyond their regular roles and full workloads to assist with this project, as well as to Vicky Kruckeberg for her careful proofreading.

The field owes much to Jane C. Nylander, Historic New England's president emerita, for all that she has contributed and continues to contribute to the understanding of New England's material culture. More personally, I am grateful to Jane for allowing me to be her novice writing partner in 2000 and for having given me the opportunity to join the Historic New England staff in 1995. I continue to learn every day that I'm here.

To President and CEO Carl R. Nold, my sincere thanks for a thoughtful introduction to this second edition and for leading Historic New England into its second century with such energy and vision. I share Carl's belief that we can be the best heritage organization in the nation.

I thank Stephen Pekich for his skillful guidance through the maze of publishing rights. It also has been a pleasure to work again with Diane Maddex of Archetype Press and its designer, Robert L. Wiser. You are true professionals.

Diane L. Viera

Page numbers in italics indicate illustrations.

Adam, Robert, 75
Adams, John, 9
Adams, John Quincy, 180
American Bicentennial, 14, 15
The American Builder's Companion (Benjamin), 76
Andrew, A. Piatt, 139, *189*
Appleton, William Sumner, 10, 12, 14, 15, 21, 67, 212, 214, 215
The Architecture of Country Houses (Downing), 80, 100
Arnold House, 215, *228*

Badger, John, 154
Barrell, Elizabeth and Mary, 90, 130, 174, 185, 198, *199*, 215
Barrett, George and Elizabeth, family, 128, 165
Barrett House (Forest Hall), *7, 8, 31, 37,* 128, *164,* 165, *168, 228*
Bateman, Peter and William, 179
Bauhaus, 61, 64, 190, 215
Beauport (Sleeper-McCann House), *16, 132–33, 136–37, 138–39, 152, 153, 153, 188, 189, 189, 206,* 207, 208, *209,* 215, *228;* servants, 136, 139, 140
Beecher, Catherine, 181
Bell, William, 51

Benjamin, Asher, 76, 222
Blackburn, Joseph, 89
The Blithedale Romance (Hawthorne), 36
Boardman, Langley, 99
Boardman, Offin, Sr., family, 121, 177
Boardman, William, family, 67, 68, 83
Boardman (William) House, *66,* 67, *67, 228*
Boston Daily Advertiser, 192, 194
Boston Sunday Globe, 216
Bowen, Henry Chandler and Ellen, family, 15, 55, 56, 80, 124, 128, 156, 170, 182, *183*
Bowen House. *See* Roseland Cottage
Bradlee family, 201
Brainerd, Eleanor Hoyt, 134
Brazer, Esther Stevens, 70
Breuer, Marcel, 64, 190
The British Architect (Swan), 71, 72
Browne, Herbert, 58, 106
Browne House, 214, *228*
The Builder's Companion (Pain), 71
Bulfinch, Charles, 75, 76, 97
Bulletin of the Society for the Preservation of New England Antiquities, 12
Byron, Lord, 208

Casey, Thomas Lincoln, 47
Casey family, 47, 55, 128, 160

Casey Farm, *30,* 44, *46, 48, 47,* 128, *160,* 215, *228*
Castle Tucker, *32, 38,* 44, 100, *100,* 122, *122, 123, 134, 135,* 135–36, *148–49,* 154, *154–55,* 156, *156, 158,* 159, *163, 169,* 170, *172–73,* 182, 186, *229;* servants, 135, 136
Cates, Henry, 154
Cawley, Delia, 143
Centennial Exhibition (1876), 194
Child, Lydia Maria, 181
Clemence-Irons House, *229*
Clifford, Ebenezer, 94
Codman, John, 48, 51, 56, 103, 127
Codman, Ogden, Jr., 56, 102, 105, 127, *127,* 201
Codman, Ogden, Sr., and Sarah, family, 56, 103, 105, 106, 110, 124, 127, *127,* 128, 149, 165, 181, 201
Codman Estate (The Grange), 18, *26,* 29, *38,* 48, *48–49,* 56, 57, 61, 102, 103, *103, 104–5,* 105, 110, *126,* 127, *127, 146–47,* 165, 166, *189,* 201, *229*
Coffin, Tristram, Jr., and Judith, family, 85, 86, 87, 89, 106, 113, 128, 150, 177, *197, 197*

Coffin House, *40, 84–85, 85, 86, 86–87, 87,* 89, 93, 106, *112–13, 113,* 150, *150–51,* 156, *157,* 159, 160, *161,* 174, *176–77, 196–97, 197, 229*
Cogswell, Jonathan, family, 70, 71
Cogswell, William, 207
Cogswell (William) House, *207*
Cogswell's Grant, 44, *45,* 70, *70,* 71, *195,* 207, 212, *212, 213, 229*
Cook, Eliza, 35
Coolidge, Nancy, 17
Cooper-Frost-Austin House, *229*
Copley, John Singleton, 200
The Country Builder's Assistant (Benjamin), 76
Winslow Crocker House, *210–11,* 211, *230*
Cummings, Abbott Lowell, 17, 153, 215
Currier and Ives, 203

Dearing, Ebenezer, 72
The Decoration of Houses (Wharton and Codman), 105
Deephaven (Jewett), 30, 39, 185, 212
Diderot, Denis, 10
Dole-Little House, *230*
Downing, Andrew Jackson, 55, 80, 100
Dudley, William Perry, 14, 208
du Pont, Henry Francis, 140, 153

Durgin (or Durkin), Bridget, 144
Dyer, Henry A., 55

Eliot, Charles W., 10
Emerson, Ralph Waldo, 26
Emmet, Alan, 43
Encyclopédie (Diderot), 10
Extown Farm, *21*

Fernald, George Porter, 58, 204
Fields, Annie, 147
Fisher, Alvan, 51
Flynn, Cornelius, 144
Foster, William, 97
Fowler House, 219
Franklin, Benjamin, 9, 10, 208, *209*
Frederick, Christine, 135

Gardner, Isabella Stewart, *189,* 207, *207*
Gedney House, *230*
Gilman, John, 14
Gilman Garrison House, *12–13, 68–69,* 208, *208, 230*
Godey's Lady's Book, 35
Goodwin family, 58, 110
Gore, Christopher and Rebecca, 22, 48, 179
Gore, John, 198
Gore Place, 22, 48
Gould family, 47
Grant, Ulysses S., 124
Griffin Farm, *220–21*
Gropius, Walter and Ise, 15, 61, 63, 64, 83, 170, 190, 215
Gropius House, *6, 33, 35, 60–61,* 61, *62–63,* 64, *64–65,* 106, *170–71, 171, 190, 191, 230*

Haggins, John, 72
Hamilton, Jonathan, 58, 203
Hamilton House, *1,* 24, *25, 29, 39,* 58, *58–59,* 106, 110, *110–11,* 149, *149,* 185, *202,* 203, *203, 204–5,* 207, 215, *230*
Hampton Court, England, 51, 185
Hancock, Thomas, 12
John Hancock House, 12, 14
Harrison, Benjamin, *182*
Sally Hart House, 204
Hasbrouck House, 14
Hawthorne, Nathaniel, opposite 1, 36
Herrick, Christine Terhune, 133
Historic New England, 10, 11, 14–15, 18, 19, 20, 21, 44, 61, 75, 212, 214, 215; stewardship easement program, 20, 216–27
Holley-Williams House, 222, 223
Holmes, Oliver Wendell, 10
Hoover House, *226–27, 227*
House and Garden, 63
House Beautiful, 207
The House of the Seven Gables (Hawthorne), opposite 1
The House Servant's Directory (Roberts), 179, 181
Household Engineering: Scientific Management in the Home (Frederick), 135

Housekeeping Made Easy (Herrick), 133
Huse family, 150, 156

Indian Hill, 207
Irving and Casson, 83

Jackson House, *66, 166, 231*
Jacobs Farm, *220*
James, P. D., 140
Jefferson, Thomas, 78, 99
Jewett, Sarah Orne, 30, 39, 58, 72, 106, 147, 149, 185, *192–93*, 198, 200, *203*, 212, 215
Sarah Orne Jewett House, 72, *73*, 93, *93*, 106–7, 184, *192–93*, 231
Johnson, Samuel, 10

Keller, Helen, *128*

Ladies' Home Journal, 134
Lafayette, Marquis de, 208, *209*
Langdon, John and Elizabeth, family, 72, 82, 83, 93, *94, 94*, 100, 106, 117, 128
Governor John Langdon House, *7, 27*, 72, *72, 82, 82–83, 83*, 94, *94, 94–95, 116–17, 117*, 128, *231*; servants, 117
Little, Amelia and Agnes, 186, 215
Little, Bertram K. and Nina Fletcher, 194, 212, 215
Longfellow, Henry Wadsworth, 33

Low, Daniel, 143
Lowell, James Russell, 9, 10
Lyman, Arthur and Ella, family, *108–9*, 110, 124, 185, 201
Lyman, Theodore, 51, 180
Lyman Estate (The Vale), *7, 11, 29, 36, 50*, 51, *51*, 110, 185, 201, *201, 231*
Lyman House (Boston), *108–9*, 124

MacLeish, Archibald, 29
Manners Culture and Dress of the Best of American Society (Wells), 143
Marcotte, Leon, 103, 105
Marrett, Daniel, family, 52, 79, 80, 128, 150, 160, 185, *185*
Marrett House, *7, 36, 78, 79*, 128, 149, 160, 161, *162–63, 163, 231*
Massachusetts Society for Promoting Agriculture (MSPA), 48, 51
May, James Rundlet, family, 128, 201
McCall's, 190, *190*
McCann, Helena Woolworth, family, 208
McCord, David, 11
McIntire, Samuel, 36, 51
McKim, Mead, and White, 82–83
Merrell Tavern, *216–17*, 219
Merwin House, *165, 231*
Mills, Richard, 72
Mount Vernon, 14

Nickels, William, 76
Nickels-Sortwell House, *2–3*, 76, *76*, 77, 190, *190, 232*
Norwood-Hyatt House, *218–19*

O'Hara, Patrick, 144, *144*
Old South Meeting House, 14
Otis, Harrison Gray and Sally, family, 75, 93, 97, 100, 106, 118, *118*, 180, 181
Harrison Gray Otis House, *36, 74–75, 75*, 76, *96–97, 97, 118, 119, 180, 180–81, 181*, 215, *232*; servants, 117

Pain, William, 71, 76
Parloa, Maria, 186
Peirce, Daniel, Jr., 68
Phillips, Anna and Stephen Willard, family, 140–41, 143, 144, *144*
Phillips, Wendell, 10
Phillips House, *19, 19, 38*, 140, 141, *142–43, 143, 144–45, 232*; servants, 140, 141, 143, 144
Pierce, Edward, 71
Pierce House, *232*
The Practical House Carpenter (Pain), 76

Quincy, Josiah, Sr., family, 71, 93, 177, 200, *200*
Quincy House, 71, *71, 92–93*, 93, 177, 200, *200–201, 232*

Rantoul, William, 140
Red Roof, 139
Roberts, Robert, 179, 181
Rocky Hill Meeting House, *33, 41, 232*
Roseland Cottage, *15, 34, 54–55, 55*, 56, 80, *80, 80–81, 100–101*, 124, *124–25*, 159, *159*, 160, 163, *163*, 165, 166, 170, 182, *182, 183*, 215, *233*
Rumford, Count, 153, 154, 159
Rundlet, James and Jane, family, 52, 93, 99, 100, 106, 121, 124, 154, 179, 181
Rundlet-May House, 52, *53, 98–99, 99, 120–21, 121*, 128, *128–29*, 154, *154*, 159, 160, *161*, 166, *166–67*, 169, *178–79, 179*, 201, *233*

Sampson-Gifford House, 219
Sanford-Covell House, 219, *219, 224, 225*
Savage, Edward, 94
Sayward, Jonathan, family, *88*, 89, 90, 93, 106, 114, *114*, 117, 130, 150, 174, 198, *198*. *See also* Barrell, Elizabeth and Mary; Wheeler, Elizabeth Cheever
Sayward-Wheeler House, *15, 88, 89*, 90, *90–91*, 114, *114–15*, 130, *130–31*, 149, 174, *174, 175*, 198, *198–99*, 215, *233*; servants, 117

Sewall, Samuel, 89
Shaughnessy, Catherine, 141, 143, 144, *144*
Short House, 219
A Sketch of the History of Newbury, Newburyport, and West Newbury (Coffin), 197
Sleeper, Henry Davis, 17, 136, 139, 140, 153, 189, *189*, 207, *207*, 208, 211
Smith, Adam, 10
Society for the Preservation of New England Antiquities (SPNEA), 10, 12, 14, 15, 216, 219. *See also* Historic New England
Sortwell family, 190, *190*
Spaulding Cooperage, 220
Spencer-Peirce-Little Farm, *22–23*, 44, *44*, 121, 160, *170*, 186, *233*
Spencer-Peirce-Little House, *endleaves*, 68, *68*, 174, *186–87, 214*
Spring, James W., 85
Storer, Bellamy and Maria, *189*
Sturgis, John Hubbard, 102, 103
Swan, Abraham, 71, 72
Swett-Ilsley House, *233*

Thacher, Mary, family, 211, *211*
Thompson, Benjamin. *See* Rumford, Count
Thoreau, Henry David, 25, 40

Tracy, Nathaniel, family, 174, 177
A Treatise on Domestic Economy (Beecher), 181
A Treatise on the Theory and Practice of Landscape Gardening (Downing), 55
Tucker, Richard, Jr., and Mollie, family, 100, 122, *122*, 128, 135–36, 154, 156, 159, 165, 174, 182, 186
Tyson, Emily and Elise, 58, 106, 185, 203, *203, 204*, 207, 215

Walpole, Horace, 208
Washington, George and Martha, 14, 117
Watson Farm, *4–5, 6, 28*, 44, *233*
The Wealth of Nations (Smith), 10
Wells, Joseph Collins, 80, 163
Wells, Richard A., 143
Wharton, Edith, 105
Wheeler, Elizabeth Cheever, family, 130
Whidden, Michael, 72
Whitefield, Edwin, 86
Whitman, Sarah Wyman, 106
Whitman, Walt, 10
Winterthur Museum, 153
Wonson, George Marble II, 139
Wonson, Mary Landergan, 136, *139*, 139–40
Woodbury, Marcia Oakes, 185

Second edition

Published by Historic New England, 141 Cambridge Street, Boston, MA 02114. Tel. 617-227-3956. www.HistoricNewEngland.org

Produced by Archetype Press, Inc.: Diane Maddex, Project Director; Gretchen Smith Mui, Editor; Carol Kim, Editorial Assistant; Robert L. Wiser, Designer

All color photographs are by David Bohl, except for pages 19, 36 (bottom right), 38 (bottom left), 74–75, 97, 132–33, 136–37, 138–39, 140, 141, 142–43, 143, 144–45, 228 (middle right), and 232 (top right), which are by David Carmack; page 220 (both), by Joseph Cornish; page 6 (bottom), by Peter Harholdt; page 228 (top right), by Daniel Nystedt; page 223 (top right), by Wendy Price; page 228 (bottom right), by Dana Salvo; pages 6 (top), 228 (top left), and 232 (bottom left), by Aaron Usher.

Library of Congress Cataloging-in-Publication Data
Nylander, Jane C.
    Windows on the past : four centuries of New England homes / Jane C. Nylander with Diane Viera ; Historic New England ; color photographs by David Bohl ; foreword by Wendell Garrett
        p. cm.
    ISBN 978-0-615-29813-9 (hardcover)
    1. Historical museums—New England. 2. Historic buildings—New England. 3. Dwellings—New England—History. 4. New England—Social life and customs. 5. New England—Antiquities—Collection and preservation. 6. Historical museums—New England—Pictorial works. 7. Historic buildings—New England—Pictorial works. 8. Dwellings—New England—Pictorial works. I. Viera, Diane. II. Society for the Preservation of New England Antiquities. III. Title.
    F5 N95 2000
    974—dc21   99-049516

Printed in Singapore

Grateful acknowledgment is made for use of the following photographs and quotations. *Photographs:* Page 72, bottom left: Courtesy Boston Athenaeum. Page 189, bottom, and page 207, top: Courtesy A. Piatt Andrew Archive. Pages 192–93: BMS AM 1743.26 by permission of the Houghton Library, Harvard University. *Quotations:* Page 29 From "Immortal Autumn," *Collected Poems 1917–1982* by Archibald MacLeish; copyright © 1985 by The Estate of Archibald MacLeish; reprinted by permission of Houghton Mifflin Harcourt Publishing Company; all rights reserved. Page 71: Courtesy Massachusetts Historical Society. Pages 114 and 117 (Sayward diary quotations): Courtesy American Antiquarian Society. Page 117 (Langdon furnishings and contract quotations): Courtesy Strawbery Banke. Page 118: Courtesy Massachusetts Historical Society.

Case binding: "Green Worm," an English wallpaper installed in 1809 in the Rundlet-May House. Endleaves: Graffiti in the attic of the Spencer-Peirce-Little House. Page 1: The Hamilton House and its garden in winter. Pages 2–3: The Nickels-Sortwell House. Pages 4–5: Some of the flock at the Watson Farm. Pages 6–7: (top, left to right) the Watson Farm, the greenhouse at the Lyman Estate, and the Barrett House; (bottom, left to right) the Gropius House, the Governor John Langdon House, and the Marrett House.